BE A BETTER PROBLEM SOLVER

Published by:
Lotus Press : Publishers & Distributors

Be a Better Problem Solver

B.K. Pathak

Lotus
PRESS

4735/22, Prakash Deep Building
Ansari Road, Darya Ganj,
New Delhi-110002

Lotus Press : Publishers & Distributors
Unit No. 220, 2nd Floor, 4735/22, Prakash Deep Building,
Ansari Road, Darya Ganj, New Delhi- 110002
Ph.: 32903912, 23280047 • E-mail : lotus_press@sify.com
www.lotuspress.co.in

Be a Better Problem Solver

ISBN: 978-81-8382-278-7

Published by : **Lotus Press : Publishers & Distributors** New Delhi-110002
Printed at : Concept Imprint, Delhi

PREFACE

Solving problems is a huge part of business success. Some business leaders thrive on managing problems, others don't. But what makes some leaders so much more successful at it than others? Is it the techniques they adopt, the advisors they hire, or maybe the staff they deploy? In reality it is a combination of all these factors, with a heavy emphasis on focus. The ability to focus on problems for what they are—nothing more, nothing less—just issues that require objective and realistic thinking and action to be solved.

There are several different ways of problem-solving–all with their own advantages and disadvantages. The process an individual adopts as a manager will be influenced by organizational policies, the kind of information available about the problem and his/her own personality and communicative style. Good problem-solving skills empower managers in their professional and personal lives. Good problem-solving skills seldom come naturally; they are consciously learnt and nurtured.

This book, *Be a Better Problem Solver,* focuses on how the management personnel can develop approaches and strategies that will enable them to effectively solve problems in a variety of contexts. It will help busy managers arrive at solutions that are both practical and effective by using simple techniques to recognize and define problems; wide range of problem-solving tools and practical techniques to solve problems in groups.

B. K. Pathak

CONTENTS

1

WHAT IS PROBLEM-SOLVING?

Problem-solving is a key skill, and it's one that can make a huge difference to your career. At work, problems are at the center of what many people do every day. You're either solving a problem for a client (internal or external), supporting those who are solving problems, or discovering new problems to solve.

Problem-solving is a mental process that involves discovering, analysing and solving problems. The ultimate goal of problem-solving is to overcome obstacles and find a solution that best resolves the issue.

The way in which people solve problems best depends largely on the unique situation. In some cases, people are better off learning everything they can about the issue and then using factual knowledge to come up with a solution. In other cases, creativity and insight are the best options.

The problems you face can be large or small, simple or complex, and easy or difficult to solve. Regardless of the nature of the problems, a fundamental part of every manager's role is finding ways to solve them. So, being a confident problem-solver is really important to your success.

Much of that confidence comes from having a good process to use when approaching a problem. With one, you can solve problems quickly and effectively. Without one, your solutions may be ineffective, or you'll get stuck and do nothing, with sometimes painful consequences.

WHAT IS A PROBLEM?

1. A problem is an opportunity for improvement.

"Every problem has a gift for you in its hands," says Richard Bach. Someone coined the word "probortunity" – an acronym combining the words "problem" and "opportunity". A probortunity is a reminder to look at problems as possible opportunities. An optimist looks at challenging or problematic events as potential opportunities for improvement. He is seen always seeking answers for the questions such as:

— Is there more than one probortunity?

— Is it my personal probortunity? Is it the organization's probortunity?

— Is it an actual probortunity or just an annoyance?

— Is this the real probortunity, or merely a symptom of a larger one?

2. A problem is the difference between the actual state and desired state.

A problem could also be the result of the knowledge that there is a gap between the actual and desired or ideal state of objectives. Clarity of the problem is determined by the clarity of the knowledge of what precisely one wants and what one has. Greater clarity of the problem helps in finding a better and effective solution.

3. A problem results from the recognition of a present imperfect and the belief in the possibility of a better future.

The belief that one's hopes can be achieved will give one

the will to aim towards a better future. Hopes challenge one's potential, and challenge is another definition of a problem.

CONFRONTED A PROBLEM

When confronted with a problem, according to Robert Harris, people are likely to adopt either of the two approaches—spot it or mop it.

1. Stop It

A stop-it approach seeks to solve a problem, so that the problem no longer exists. Its three forms are prevention, elimination, and reduction.

1. *Prevent It.* Preventing a problem from occurring or recurring is the most ideal solution. The prevention approach is often a difficult one to apply because it requires predictive foresight ("this might be a problem someday if we don't act now"). For example, by preventing a cold, or an automobile accident, one can avoid the need to deal any further with a problem or its effects.
2. *Eliminate It.* Eliminating a problem once and for all is also an ideal way of attacking a problem. If a tank were leaking, an elimination solution would be to plug/seal or otherwise repair the leak, the cause of the problem. To solve by eliminating should be considered in nearly every problem situation.
3. *Reduce It.* The magnitude of any problem can be lessened by reducing its size. Suppose the tank is leaking and a repair (an elimination-solution) is not possible until a day or two later. The problem could be reduced by turning off the incoming water. Without line pressure on the tank, the leak

would slow down; that would be better than a full force leak.

2. Mop It

A mop-it approach focuses on the effects of a problem. Instead of treating the leak itself, the water on the floor is mopped up—the effects of the problem.

1. *Treat It.* Here the damage caused by the problem is repaired or treated. The water on the floor is mopped up and the damaged floor is fixed. But, it should be noted that: (*a*) by itself a treat-it solution is not going to be nearly as effective as some form of stop-it solution and (*b*) treat-it solutions are often needed in addition to an elimination or reduction form of solution.
2. *Tolerate It.* In this form of mop-it approach, the effects of the problem are put up with. In the leaky water example, one might install a drain in the floor, or waterproof the floor. The effects are taken for granted and measures are taken to endure them.
3. *Redirect It.* Here the problem is deflected. Sometimes the problem will simply be redefined as not a problem. It is hard to think of a legitimate redirection for the leaking water problem, but suppose that the leak is small and the floor is not being damaged. One might say, "Well, I need the humidity; the leak is actually a good thing." It should be remembered that a problem is a problem only when someone defines it as such.

CAUSES OF INEFFECTIVE PROBLEM-SOLVING

Ineffective or poor problem-solving can be the result of any of the following factors. These factors act like blinkers, constricting the perspective of person in the process of problem-solving.

Bounded Rationality

Propounded by Herbert Simon, the concept of bounded rationality assumes that individuals make decisions by constructing simplified models that extract the essential features from problems without capturing all their complexity. Simon remarks that a majority of the people are only partly rational, and are in fact emotional/ irrational in the remaining part of their actions. He indicates two major causes of bounded rationality:

1. Limitations of the human mind.
2. The structure within which the mind operates.

He states that boundedly rational people experience limits in formulating and solving problems. As a result, when calculating expected utility, people do not make the best choices.

For example, a person may choose to buy a particular brand of new cell-phone, based on the information he gathered from advertisements and friends. Constrained by bounded rationality, he will turn down even if he is offered a better bargain. Often, bounded rationality could also be caused by "inverted intelligence"—clever people who can easily argue that the information must be wrong.

Satisficing

Satisficing implies identifying and implementing a solution that is "good enough." According to Herb Simon, who coined the term, the tendency to 'satisfice' results in solving problems which do not lead to optimal solutions. Most often, people look for solutions that had worked for them before. There may be better ways to reach the outcome, but they simply ignore them. Searching for alternative and superior solutions might entail an extra cost. The alternative solution might not prove worthy enough, if the extra costs are not justified. On the other hand, the implicit costs of ignoring the alternative solution can be relatively greater if the chosen solution, based on prior experience, fails to deliver the expected outcome.

Michael Slote gives the following examples of satsificing. One involves a fairy-tale hero who, when rewarded by the gods with whatever he asks for, just asks for himself and his family to be comfortably well-off. Another involves a hotel owner who gives some stranded motorists the first available room rather than the best available room.

Groupthink

'Groupthink' is a term coined by psychologist Irving Janis. 'Groupthink' is a phenomenon in which the norm for consensus overrides the realistic appraisal of alternative courses of action. It describes situations in which group pressures for conformity discourage the group from critically appraising unusual, minority, or unpopular views. 'Groupthink' is a bug that strikes groups and can dramatically hinder their performance.

Some of the symptoms of 'Groupthink' are:

- *Illusion of Invulnerability*: Members ignore obvious danger, take extreme risk and are overly optimistic.
- *Collective Rationalization*: Members discredit and explain away warning contrary to group thinking.
- *Illusion of Morality*: Members believe their decisions are morally correct, ignoring the ethical consequences of their decisions.
- *Excessive Stereotyping*: The group constructs negative stereotypes of rivals outside the group.

- *Pressure for Conformity*: Members pressure any in the group who express arguments against the group's stereotypes, illusions, or commitments, viewing such opposition as disloyalty.
- *Self-Censorship*: Members withhold their dissenting views and counterarguments.
- *Illusion of Unanimity*: Members perceive falsely that everyone agrees with the group's decision; silence is seen as consent.
- *Mindguards*: Some members appoint themselves to the role of protecting the group from adverse information that might threaten group complacency.

Groupshift

'Groupshift' is a phenomenon in which the initial positions of individual members of a group are exaggerated toward a more extreme position. More often, however, the shift is toward greater risk. What happens in groups is that the discussion leads to a significant shift in the positions of members toward a more extreme position in the direction in which they were already leaning before the discussion. Conservatives become more cautious, and the more aggressive take on more risk.

The 'Groupshift' can be viewed as actually a special case of 'groupthink'. The decision of the group reflects the dominant decision-making norm that develops during the group's discussion. The greater occurrence of the shift toward risk can be due to any of the following reasons:

- Discussion creates familiarization among the members. As they become more comfortable with each other, they also become more bold and daring.

– People admire individuals who are willing to take risks. Group discussion motivates members to show that they are at least as willing as their peers in terms of taking risks.
– The most plausible explanation of the shift toward risk, however, seems to be that the group diffuses responsibility.
– Group decisions free any single member from accountability for the group's final choice.

Conformation Bias

Conformation bias is the tendency on the part of the people to search for only for that information that supports their perceived notions. Initial perceptions and ideas of people about a problem often shape the search process for information. It is important to maintain objectivity in evaluating ideas so that they are not biased toward their initial perceptions. The possible solutions include:

– Considering alternative hypotheses—view the problem from different perspectives.
– Looking for evidence to disprove their ideas—showing that a particular idea is incorrect is as important as showing an idea is correct.
– Maintain objectivity while evaluating ideas to minimise personal bias.
– Drawing conclusions based upon the evidence, not upon their personal beliefs.

Insufficiency of Hypotheses

Often, while solving problems, a solver seizes upon the first explanation that comes to mind and stops thinking about the problem. This difficulty is related to confirmation bias, but reflects insufficient thought applied to a problem. Many times, the immediate answer is sufficient. Other times, however, only a careful analysis of a situation beyond the immediate response is necessary to ensure a correct solution. To avoid poor problem-solving resulting from insufficiency of hypothesis, people should develop alternative ideas, rather than seizing upon the first idea as the solution.

Fixation

Fixation is the inability to see a problem from a fresh perspective. Again, initial perceptions and structuring of a problem often determine the approaches people use to solve that problem. Structuring a problem incorrectly is a prime contributor to the inability to solve a problem correctly. To overcome fixation, people should see the problem with "fresh eyes"—allow time for reflection and incubation. They should focus on other issues, and then return to the original problem. Time away from a problem allows one to forget incorrect solutions and focus on developing new ideas.

Other Obstacles

Problem-solving can be impaired by biases of personal beliefs, a misunderstanding of information relevant to solving problems, and overconfidence. The solution is to study a problem objectively with all available accurate information and use objective reasoning to achieve a reasonable, sound decision. People should be sure that they understand the problem and find what constitutes a solution. They should obtain as much accurate and comprehensive information from unbiased sources possible and maintain objectivity in evaluating ideas to minimise personal bias. They should assess their decisions critically and be able to defend their ideas.

PROBLEM-SOLVING SKILLS FOR MANAGERS

Managers must take cognizance of the fact that problem-solving is an ongoing activity. Prof. Jeff Malpas says: "No problem is ever totally solved. Every problem has a solution, but every solution with it brings a new problem. Some well-known management techniques emphasize the idea of continuous improvement and successful problem-solving is seen as part of such continuous improvement."

Managers should know that problem-solving is less a matter of continuous improvement as of continuous adjustment. Every solution will have unintended consequences. Every effective system gives rise to friction and failure. Good management and effective problem-solving depend upon a willingness to adapt to the situation and recognise the ongoing and partial character of all attempts to manage or to solve.

Sometimes, as we look for approaches to creative thinking, we forget that many of the most powerful techniques are also the simplest. Leonardo da Vinci, one of the most creative thinkers in history, says of his inspiration:

> "I roamed the countryside searching for answers to things I did not understand. Why shells exist on the tops of mountains along with imprints of plants usually found in the sea. Why thunder lasts longer than that which causes it. How circles of water form around the spot which has been struck by a stone. And how a bird suspends itself in the air. Questions like these engaged my thought throughout my life".

It is easy to forget, as we rush through our lives, that curiosity is an essential foundation for creativity.

Good problem-solving skills empower managers in their professional and personal lives. Good problem-solving skills seldom come naturally; they are consciously learnt and nurtured. The repertoire of good problem-solving skills includes:

- developing creative and innovative solutions;
- developing practical solutions;
- showing independence and initiative in identifying problems and solving them;
- applying a range of strategies to problem-solving;
- applying problem-solving strategies across a range of areas.

Good problem-solvers have a systematic approach to solving the problem. They understand that quick solutions or hastily conceived plans rarely work and yield results that are short-term, at best. Spend time analysing the problem from all possible angles. Come up with a backup plan, in case the original idea fails.

Consider, for example, a situation that managers sometimes face: A job applicant they are seriously considering asks for a higher salary. One option is to offer the candidate an alternative, like tuition reimbursement or location in another office. The candidate might actually re-think his or her position and trade in the demand for a higher salary for potential career growth.

Instances like this show that negotiation is a useful tool for problem-solving. Negotiations call for making decisions, but decision-making styles vary from one person to another and from one organization to another. It is often the culture of the organization that determines the style of making decisions.

Good executives expect crisis and are prepared for it. The crisis may be the result of bad employee relations, poor products or outdated technology. Whatever the case, however, the scenario is anticipated and the plan of action thought out ahead of time. This rule can come in handy for anyone, whether just starting a career or at a senior level.

Some rules to keep in mind when solving problems: Maintain an open and honest communication with the people involved and do not resort to personal attacks or finger- pointing. Observe how your supervisor tackles a tricky situation. This will also help you gain valuable insights into ways your organization functions.

❖❖❖

2

APPROACHES TO PROBLEM-SOLVING

Regardless of what they do for a living or where they live, most people spend most of their waking hours, at work or at home, solving problems. Most problems we face are small, some are large and complex, but they all need to be solved in a satisfactory way.

A problem can be a real break, the stroke of luck, opportunity knocking, a chance to get out of the rut of the everyday and make yourself or some situation better. Note that problems need not arrive as a result of external factors or bad events. Any new awareness you have that allows you to see possibilities for improvement brings a "problem" for you to solve. This is why the most creative people are "problem seekers" rather than "problem avoiders."

Developing a positive attitude toward problems can transform you into a happier, saner, more confident person who feels (and is) much more in control of life. Train yourself to respond to problems with enthusiasm and eagerness, rising to the opportunity to show your stuff, and you will be amazed at the result.

In our ordinary discourse, we often think of "solving a problem" in the sense of making it go away, so that the problem no longer exists. This indeed is one kind of solution, but it is not the only kind. Some problems cannot be eliminated entirely: we are never likely to eliminate trash, or the wear on automobile tyres, or the occurrence of illness. We can, however, create solutions or treatments that will make each of these problems less harmful.

For our purposes, then, we will define a solution as the management of a problem in a way that successfully meets the goals established for treating it. Sometimes the goal will be to eliminate the problem entirely; sometimes the goal will be only to treat the effects of the problem. The possibilities inherent in the problem, together with the ambitiousness, resources, and values of the problem-solver, will help to shape the goals.

There are several different ways of problem-solving – all have their own advantages and disadvantages. The process an individual adopts as a manager will be influenced by organizational policies, the kind of information available about the problem and his/ her own personality and communicative style. Broadly, there are three problem-solving models available to a manager.

RATIONAL PROBLEM-SOLVING

The brain can think in two ways—emotionally (governed by instinctive feelings) and rationally (governed by acquired knowledge and beliefs).

Emotional thinking happens in the limbic system—an interconnected system of brain nuclei associated with basic needs and emotions, for example, hunger, pain, pleasure, satisfaction, sex, and instinctive motivation"). When something catches one's attention, the brain, in a lightning flash, looks through all the inherited and remembered patterns to see if there is a match, and responds with the closest pattern that it can find. Emotional thinking is very clear-cut, black and white, all or nothing. For example, when a black shape on the path looks like a snake, one feels frightened and runs away.

Rational thinking, on the other hand, is a function of the part of the brain called the neocortex—the wrinkled outer layer of the front parts of the brain (the cerebral hemispheres), the functions of which include the perception of sensations, learning, reasoning and memory. The power to think rationally gives an individual greater flexibility of response. One has a lot more control over what one does. So that one realises that the black shape on the path, though it looks like a snake, could also be a stick, examines it more closely before deciding what to do.

Rational problem-solving rests on the following principles:

1. Problems are identified by comparing actual performance with an expected standard performance.
2. Problems are deviations in actual performance from the expected standard.
3. A precise and complete description of the problem is needed to identify a solution:
   a) What is happening?
   b) Where is it happening?
   c) When is it happening?
   d) To what extent is it happening?
4. The cause of the problem will be found by comparing problem and non-problem situations.
5. Recent problems are a result of some change in the situation that has caused an unwanted deviation from expectations.

The Rational Decision-Making Model requires the following steps which, if followed, are assumed to lead to "value-maximising choices." The steps are as follows:

1. Define the problem,
2. Identify the decision criteria,
3. Weigh the criteria to determine rank of importance,
4. Generate possible alternative solutions,
5. Rate each alternative on each criteria, and
6. Compute the optimal decision.

The case again rational problem-solving is the flawed assumption that every problem is defined clearly and precisely, which might not be always possible. Also, rating each of the alternative problem-solutions relatively in terms of set or predetermined criteria can be a tricky task.

LATERAL OR CREATIVE PROBLEM-SOLVING

During 1950 -1960, some significant research was done by Roger Sperry, which won him the Nobel Prize for Medicine in 1981. Sperry's work demonstrated that human brain is divided into two major parts or hemispheres—the right brain and the left brain.

The left brain is associated with verbal, logical, and analytical thinking. It excels in naming and categorizing things, symbolic abstraction, speech, reading, writing and arithmetic. The left brain is very linear: it places things in sequential order—first things first and then second things second, etc. Left brain engages in a very systematic, sequential and exact approach to getting the job done. The left brain strives for accuracy in the process of the job being done.

The right brain, on the other hand, functions in a non-verbal manner and excels in visual, spatial, perceptual, and intuitive information. It is associated with the realm of creativity. The right brain processes information differently than the left brain. The processing happens very quickly and the style of processing is non-linear and non-sequential. The right brain looks at the whole picture and quickly seeks to determine the spatial relationships of all the parts as they relate to the whole. This component of the brain is not concerned with things falling into patterns because of prescribed rules.

So, lateral or creative problem-solving does not follow a standard set of procedures. It is a 'subconscious process based on past distilled experiences'. It is based more on the gut feeling of the manager than on an objective process of weighing alternatives. There are a set of conditions and it is accepted that under those conditions intuitive approach is generally preferred to rational approach. Intuitive method is preferred when:

1. A high level of uncertainty exists,
2. There is little precedence to draw on,
3. Variables are not reliably predictable,
4. Facts are limited or facts are contradictory,
5. Analytical data are of little use,
6. There are several plausible solutions; and
7. Time is limited and decision must be made.

The Creative Problem-solving Process (CPS), also known as the Osborn-Parnes CPS process, was developed by Alex Osborn and Dr. Sidney J. Parnes in the 1950s. CPS is a structured method for generating novel and useful solutions to problems. CPS follows three process stages, which match a person's natural creative process, and six explicit steps:

Process Stage	*Steps*
Explore the Challenge	*Objective Finding* (identify the goal, wish or challenge)
	Fact Finding (gather the relevant data)
	Problem Finding (clarify the problems that need to be solved in order to achieve the goal)
Generate Ideas	*Idea Finding* (generate ideas to solve the identified problem)
Prepare for Action	*Solution Finding* (move from idea to implementable solution)
	Acceptance Finding (plan for action)

1. Objective (Mess) Finding

The problem-solver discusses the situation about the problem and brainstorms a list of objectives or goals which he/she might have for him/her creative effort. Through some process, arrive at consensus on one or more objectives the group is willing to attempt.

2. Fact Finding

The problem-solver brainstorms all the facts which might even remotely be related to the objective. She/he has made sure that each perspective and participant is represented on the listing. She/he has to take some time for the participants to point out which facts they feel are most relevant to the objective and its eventual solution.

3. Problem Finding

One of the most powerful aspects of creativity is rephrasing the problem definition to one which is both closer to the real problem and reveals more obvious solutions. One technique for this is to brainstorm different ways to state the problem. Most people recommend that the problem statement be written as: "In what ways might we..." One has to pay particular attention to changing the verbs and the nouns in the problem statement. Asking "Why?" and "How?" will also result in some interesting problem statements. Let the owner of the problem select the statement or statements which seem to best capture the "real" problem.

4. Idea Finding

In this step, the ideas with the greatest potential are evaluated and the problem owner selects an idea or set of ideas to take action on. One of the most effective methods for this step is to brainstorm the criteria which determine the best idea, like cost, appearance, etc., then select the most useful criteria. These criteria are then used in a decision matrix in which every idea is evaluated on every criterion and the judgements combined to select the idea worth putting into action.

5. Solution Finding

Uses a specific tool called "POWER" to develop the selected solution into something more robust. POWER is short for:

- *Positives*: What's good about the idea?
- *Objections*: What's bad about it?
- *What else*?: What does it remind you of?
- *Enhancements:* How can what's good about it be made better?
- *Remedies:* How can the things that are bad about it be corrected?

6. Acceptance Finding

In this phase, the problem-solvers consider the real world issues of the change from the old way to the proposed new way as well as issues that are likely to have a bearing upon the acceptance and implementation of the envisaged change. The ideas developed in this step are then integrated into the plan, increasing it's likelihood of success.

Unlike many other problem-solving methods, the process emphasizes the need to defer judgement on possible ideas and solutions until a final decision is made. In this way, the flow of ideas in the third step is not interrupted, and possible solutions, however, bizarre, are accepted.

❖❖❖

3

PROBLEM-SOLVING PROCESS

There is a variety of problem-solving processes. But each process consists of a series of steps—identifying the problem, searching for possible solutions, selecting the most optimal solution and implementing a possible solution. It is useful to view problem-solving as a cycle because, sometimes, a problem needs several attempts to solve it or the problem changes. The diagram below shows a seven-step problem-solving process.

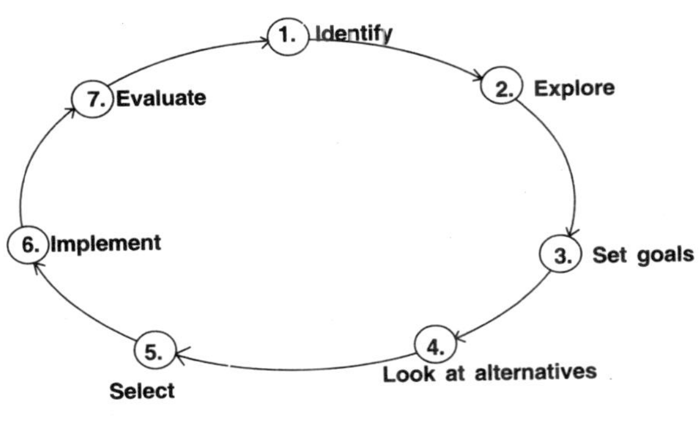

Problem-solving Process

IDENTIFYING THE PROBLEM

The first step in the problem-solving process is sizing up

the situation to identify the problem. That sounds simple enough, but sometimes managers might be uncertain about what the problem is; they might just feel general anxiety or be confused about what is getting in the way of their objectives. If that is the case, they can ask themselves or their friends or a professional expert. Other useful techniques for identifying the problem include:

- Comparison with others
- Monitor for weak signals
- Comparison of current performance with objectives or past performance
- Checklists
- Brainstorming
- Listing complaints
- Role playing

EXPLORING THE PROBLEM

Having identified the problem, managers should analyse it to see what the root cause is. Often people get caught up in symptoms or effects of a problem or issue and never get down to the real cause. They get mad at someone's attitude, anger, or actions, which are not the cause of the problem. The key here is to focus on analysing the problem for the real cause without being affected by emotional issues. Seeing answers for questions such as the following will help explore the problem:

1. Ask Who?
   - Who says that this is a problem?
   - Who caused or is causing the problem?
   - Whom does it or will it affect?
   - Who has done something about the problem?

2. Ask What?
   - What happened or will happen?
   - What are the symptoms?
   - What are the consequences for others?
   - What circumstances surround the occurrence of the problem?
   - What is not functioning as desired?
3. Ask When?
   - Did it or will it happen?
   - Why did it happen?
   - When did it first occur?
4. Ask Where?
   - Where is the problem occurring?
   - Did it or will it have an impact?
   - Where did it have an impact?
5. Ask Why?
   - Why is this, a problem?
   - Did it or will it occur?
   - Why did it occur?
   - Why was nothing done to prevent the problem from occurring?
   - Why did no one recognize and do something about the problem at the earliest?
   - Why is a response needed now?
6. Ask How?
   - How should the process be working?
   - How are others dealing with this or similar problems?
   - How do you know this is a problem; what supporting information do you have?

Once the cause is found, plans can be made to fix it. Analysing implies gathering information. If there is not enough information, they should figure out how to research and collect it

SET GOALS

Having explored and analysed the problem, managers should be able to write a goal statement that focuses on what is the successful end of the process.

Making and writing down a goal statement:

- helps them to clarify the direction to take in solving the problem; and
- gives them something definite to focus on.

That is, what will occur as a result of the solution? This whole process is about closing or fixing the gap between the problem and the goal. Writing down the problem ensures that they are not side-tracking from, but addressing the problem.

LOOK AT ALTERNATIVES

Now that the problem has been analysed, the managers can begin to develop possible solutions. This is a creative as well as practical step where every possible solution is identified. They should identify the various alternative solutions available to them through such techniques as:

- Analysis of past solutions
- Reading
- Researching
- Thinking
- Asking Questions
- Discussing

- Viewing the problem with fresh eyes
- Brainstorming
- Sleeping on it

The idea is to collect as many alternative solutions as possible.

Mind mapping is another technique that can be used for identifying alternative solutions. Developed by Tony Buzan in the 1970's, mind mapping uses pictures and/ or word phrases to organize and develop thoughts in a non-linear fashion. It helps people "see" a problem and its solution. Here's how to do mind mapping:

- Take a sheet of plain paper and turn it sideways (if using flipchart paper you don't need to turn it sideways—it is large enough); Using colored felt pens, draw a small picture (or write a phrase) in the centre of the paper representing the issue you want to solve; Draw lines out from the main problem (it helps to use different colors for each line).
- Each line should represent a different aspect of your problem or issue;
- Write down what each line represents either on top of or on the line;
- Add other lines flowing off these main lines;
- Write a word or short phrase on the smaller lines indicating what each new line represents (you may find that mind mapping works best for you if you write down the phrases or draw the images first and then connect them with the lines); and
- If you want, add images next to your main line that illustrate what each line means to you (some people think better with pictures, others with words).

SELECT THE BEST SOLUTION

Now that there are a wide variety of possible solutions, it is time to select the best solution to fix the problem, given the circumstances, resources and other considerations. Here the managers are trying to figure out exactly what would work best given the nature of the problem. There are always a number of things that can affect a solution, for instance, money, time, people, procedures, policies, rules, and so on. All of these factors must be thought about. Managers should prioritize the solutions by their effectiveness. This is a slow process of elimination. There may be some possible suggestions that are immediately eliminated. Eventually, managers should narrow down the choices to one best possible solution which will promise the best or optimal outcomes.

IMPLEMENTATION

Implementation is a crucial part of problem-solving process. In order to implement the solution chosen, managers must have an action plan and communicate it to those directly and indirectly affected. Gemmy Allen says that communication is most effective when it precedes action and events. In this way, events conform to plans and events happen when, and in the way, they should happen. Managers should answer the vital questions before they are asked, like –

- What should be communicated?
- What is the reason for the decision?
- Whom will it affect and how?
- What are the benefits expected for the individual, the department, and the organization?
- What adjustments will be required in terms of how work will be done?

- What, specifically, is each individual's role in implementing the decision?
- What results are expected from each individual?
- When does the action called for by the decision go into effect?

Communicating answers to these questions can overcome any resistance that otherwise might be encountered.

EVALUATION

This is the final step in the problem-solving process. Managers should review the effectiveness of the solution against desired outcomes. Did the solution work? If not, why not? What went right, and what went wrong? What adjustments do they have to make to ensure that the solution works better? This stage requires careful analysis that improves upon the best solution.

The review of your progress can help a manager identify any problem. Steps may need to be revised or new steps added. One may need to consider a different solution, if the current one, he/she has been working with, is not helping.

PROBLEM-SOLVING ORIENTATIONS

According to Karl Jung's *Psychological Types,* people are all different in fundamental ways. Their aptitude and competence to process different information is limited by their personality type. These types are eight in number, such as:

- People can be either Extroverts or Introverts, depending on the direction of their activity;
- Thinking, Feeling, Sensing, Intuitive, according to their own information pathways; and

— Judging or Perceiving, depending on the method in which they process received information.

Extroverts *vs.* Introverts

Extroverts are directed towards the objective world whereas Introverts are directed towards the subjective world. The most common differences between Extroverts and Introverts are shown below:

Extroverts

— are interested in what is happening around them
— are open and often talkative
— compare their own opinions with the opinions of others
— like action and initiative
— easily make new friends or adapt to a new group
— say what they think
— are interested in new people
— easily break unwanted relations

Introverts

— are interested in their own thoughts and feelings
— need to have own territory
— often appear reserved, quiet and thoughtful
— usually do not have many friends
— have difficulties in making new contacts
— like concentration and quietness
— do not like unexpected visits and therefore do not make them
— work well when alone

Sensing *vs.* Intuition

Sensing is an ability to deal with information on the basis of its physical qualities and its relation to other information. Intuition is an ability to deal with the information on the basis of its hidden potential and its possible existence. The most common differences between Sensing and Intuitive types are shown below:

Sensing types

— see everyone and sense everything
— live in the here and now
— quickly adapt to any situation
— like pleasures based on physical sensation
— are practical and active
— are realistic and self-confident

Intuitive types

— are mostly in the past or in the future
— worry about the future more than the present
— are interested in everything new and unusual
— do not like routine
— are attracted more to the theory than the practice
— often have doubts

Thinking *vs.* Feeling

Thinking is an ability to deal with information on the basis of its structure and its function. Feeling is an ability to deal with information on the basis of its initial energetic condition and its interactions. The most common differences between Thinking and Feeling type are shown below:

Thinking types

— are interested in systems, structures, patterns
— expose everything to logical analysis
— are relatively cold and unemotional
— evaluate things by intellect and right or wrong
— have difficulties talking about feelings
— do not like to clear up arguments or quarrels

Feeling types

— are interested in people and their feelings
— easily pass their own moods to others
— pay great attention to love and passion
— evaluate things by ethics and good or bad
— can be touchy or use emotional manipulation
— often give compliments to please people

Perceiving *vs.* Judging

Perceiving types are motivated into activity by the changes in a situation. Judging types are motivated into activity by their decisions resulting from the changes in a situation. The most common differences between Perceiving and Judging types are shown below:

Perceiving types

— act impulsively following the situation
— can start many things at once without finishing them properly
— prefer to have freedom from obligations
— are curious and like a fresh look at things
— work productivity depends on their mood
— often act without any preparation

Judging types

— do not like to leave questions unanswered
— plan work ahead and tend to finish it
— do not like to change their decisions
— have relatively stable workability
— easily follow rules and discipline

Researchers like Lawrence, McCaulley and Myers have investigated the relationship of Karl Jung's theory of individuals' preferences and their approach to problem-solving and decision-making. Their findings are summarized below:

1. When solving problems, individuals who are introverts will want to take time to think and clarify their ideas before they begin talking. They will more likely be concerned with their own understanding of important concepts and ideas.
2. Individuals who are extroverts will want to talk through their ideas in order to clarify them. They will continually seek feedback from the environment about the viability of their ideas.

3. Sensing individuals will be more likely to pay attention to facts, details, and reality. They will also tend to select standard solutions that have worked in the past.
4. Persons with intuition preferences will more likely attend to the meaningfulness of the facts, the relationships among the facts, and the possibilities of future events that can be imagined from these facts. They will exhibit a tendency to develop new, original solutions rather than to use what has worked previously.
5. Individuals with a thinking preference will tend to use logic and analysis during problem-solving. They are also likely to value objectivity and be impersonal in drawing conclusions. They want solutions to make sense in terms of the facts, models, and/or principles under consideration.
6. Individuals with a feeling preference are more likely to consider values and feelings in the problem-solving process. They will tend to be subjective in their decision-making and to consider how their decisions could affect other people.
7. People, particularly, the 'judging' types, are more likely to prefer structure and organization to the problems itself and will want the problem-solving process to demonstrate closure.
8. People with a perceiving preference are more likely to prefer flexibility and adaptability. They will be more concerned that the problem-solving process considers a variety of techniques and provides for unforeseen changes.

PROBLEM-SOLVING TECHNIQUES

It is not enough to describe a problem-solving process

and to describe how individuals differ in their approach to or use of it. It is also necessary to identify specific techniques of attending to individual differences. Fortunately, a variety of problem-solving techniques has been identified to accommodate individual preferences. Some of these techniques are oriented more to individuals who are more structured, more rational and analytical, and more goal-oriented in their approach to problem-solving.

Other techniques are more suited to individuals who demonstrate a preference for an approach that is more holistic and parallel, more emotional and intuitive, more creative, more visual, and more tactual/kinesthetic. It is important that techniques from both categories be selected and used in the problem-solving process.

William G. Huitt lists out the following sixteen problem-solving techniques, which focus more on logic and critical thinking, especially within the context of applying the scientific approach:

a) Means-End Analysis: In means-ends analysis, the problem-solver compares the present situation with the goal, detects a difference between them, and then searches memory for actions that are likely to reduce the difference.

b) Backwards Planning: The strategy of working backwards entails starting with the end results and reversing the steps you need to get those results, in order to figure out the answer to the problem.

c) Categorising/Classifying: It is the process of grouping objects or events together on the basis of a logical rationale. There are two kinds of categorizing, grouping and classifying. Grouping is putting together objects on the basis of a single property. Files might be grouped on the basis of "urgent" and "not-urgent". Grouping is useful in revealing similarities and differences that otherwise might go unnoticed. Classifying involves putting items together on the basis of more than a single property at a time.

d) *Challenging Assumptions*: It involves the direct confrontation of ideas, opinions, or attitudes that have previously been taken for granted. The purpose is to identify the fallacies, consistencies and inconsistencies in the problem-solving process.

e) *Evaluating/Judging*: It involves the comparison with a standard and making a qualitative or quantitative judgement of value or worth. Good evaluations of problem-solving are generally based on multiple sources of assessment information.

f) *Inductive/Deductive Reasoning*: Reasoning is the systematic and logical development of rules or concepts from specific instances or the identification of cases based on a general principle or proposition using generalisation and inference.

g) *Thinking Aloud*: It is the process of verbalising about a problem and its solution while a partner listens in detail for errors in thinking or understanding.

h) *Network Analysis*: It is a systems approach to project planning and management where relationships among activities, events, resources, and timelines are developed and charted. Specific examples include Program Evaluation and Review Technique and Critical Path Method.

i) *Plus-Minus-Interesting (PMI)*: It involves considering the positive, negative, and interesting or thought-provoking aspects of an idea or alternative using a balance sheet grid where plus and minus refer to criteria identified in the second step of the problem-solving process.

j) Task analysis: It is the consideration of skills and knowledge required to learn or perform a specific task.

Now let us take a look at Huitt's list of problem-solving techniques that conform to creative, lateral, or divergent thinking. Following is the list of problem-solving techniques:

a) Brainstorming: It is attempting to spontaneously generate as many ideas on a subject as possible; ideas are not critiqued during the brainstorming process; participants are encouraged to form new ideas from ideas already stated.

b) Imaging/Visualisation: It is producing mental pictures of the total problem or specific parts of the problem.

c) Incubation: It is putting aside the problem and doing something else to allow the mind to unconsciously consider the problem

d) Outcome Psychodrama: It is enacting a scenario of alternatives or solutions through role playing.

e) Outrageous Provocation: It is making a statement that is known to be incorrect (e.g., the brain is made of charcoal) and then considering it; used as a bridge to a new idea.

f) Overload: It is considering a large number of facts and details until the logic part of the brain becomes overwhelmed and begins looking for patterns. It can also be generated by immersion in aesthetic experiences, sensitivity training or similar experiences.

g) Random Word Technique: It is selecting a word randomly from the dictionary and juxtaposing it with problem statement, then brainstorming about possible relationships.

h) *Relaxation:* It is systematically relaxing all muscles while repeating a personally meaningful focus word or phrase.

i) *Synthesizing*: It is combining parts or elements into a new and original pattern.

j) *Taking Another's Perspective:* It is deliberately taking another person's point of view.

k) *Value Clarification:* It is using techniques such as role playing, simulations, self-analysis exercises, and structured controversy to gain a greater understanding of attitudes and beliefs that individuals hold important. The value clarification can provide a greater goal clarity and motivation and increase an internal locus of control for managers.

Useind de Bono's 'Six Thinking Hats' to improve your thinking skills

The 'Six Thinking Hats' is a quick, simple and powerful technique to improve your thinking. It does this by encouraging you to recognise what type of thinking you are using, and to apply different types of thinking to the subject.

Sounds strange? Take two minutes to expand your thinking skills...We all use different types of thinking, usually without realising it. For example, if we are feeling pessimistic about the situation, that is the only type of thinking we apply! This limits our ability to see all the issues.

- *The White Hat* is cold, neutral, and objective. Take time to look at the facts and figures.
- *The Red Hat* represents anger (seeing red). Take time to listen to your emotions, your intuition.
- *The Black Hat* is gloomy and negative. Take time to look at why this will fail.

- *The Yellow Hat* is sunny and positive. Take time to be hopeful and optimistic.
- *The Green Hat* is grass, fertile and growing. Take time to be creative and cultivate new ideas.
- *The Blue Hat* is the color of the sky, high above us all. Take time to look from a higher and wider perspective to see whether you are addressing the right issue.

You can also think of the hats as pairs: White and Red, Black and Yellow and Green and Blue.

Next time you are thinking through an issue, try on de Bono's thinking hats. You'll soon find that they give you a quick, simple, and powerful technique to improve your thinking.

Steps for Boosting Creativity

1. *Listen to favarite music.* If it doesn't make you more creative, you should probably see your doctor—or your brain surgeon if you are also troubled by headaches, hallucinations or strange urges in the middle of the night.
2. *Brainstorm.* If properly carried out, brainstorming can help you not only come up with sacks full of new ideas, but can help you decide which is best.
3. *Always carry a small notebook and a pen or pencil around with you.* That way, if you are struck by an idea, you can quickly note it down. Upon rereading your notes, you may discover about 90 per cent of your ideas are daft. Don't worry, that's normal. What's important are the 10 per cent that are brilliant.
4. *If you're stuck for an idea, open a dictionary, randomly select a word and then try to formulate ideas*

incorporating this word. You'd be surprised how well this works. The concept is based on a simple but little known truth: freedom inhibits creativity. There are nothing like restrictions to get you thinking.

5. *Define your problem.* Grab a sheet of paper, electronic notebook, computer or whatever you use to make notes, and define your problem in detail. You'll probably find ideas positively spewing out once you've done this.
6. *If you can't think, go for a walk.* A change of atmosphere is good for you and gentle exercise helps shake up the brain cells.
7. *Don't watch TV.* Experiments performed by the *JPB Creative Laboratory* show that watching TV causes your brain to slowly trickle out your ears and/or nose. It's not pretty, but it happens.
8. *Don't do drugs.* People on drugs think they are creative. To everyone else, they seem like people on drugs.
9. *Read as much as you can about everything possible.* Books exercise your brain, provide inspiration and fill you with information that allows you to make creative connections easily.
10. *Exercise your brain.* Brains, like bodies, need exercise to keep fit. If you don't exercise your brain, it will get flabby and useless. Exercise your brain by reading a lot, talking to clever people and disagreeing with people—arguing can be a terrific way to give your brain cells a workout. But note, arguing about politics or film directors is good for you; bickering over who should clean the dishes is not.

4

PROBLEM-SOLVING TOOLS

Good problem-solving skills are fundamentally important if you are going to be successful in your career. But problems are something that we don't particularly like. They are time-consuming. They muscle their way into already packed schedules. They force us to think about an uncertain future. And they never seem to go away! That's why, when faced with problems, most of us try to eliminate them as quickly as possible. But have you ever chosen the easiest or most obvious solution – and then realized that you have entirely missed a much better solution? Or have you found yourself fixing just the symptoms of a problem, only for the situation to get much worse? To be an effective problem-solver, you need to be systematic and logical in your approach.

The following are some of the principal tools that enable managers to analyse and prioritise the root causes of identified problems and to assist in problem-solving activities. The tools outlined can also assist in identifying opportunities for improvement.

CAUSE-AND-EFFECT DIAGRAM

Cause and Effect relationships govern everything that happens and as such are the paths to effective problem-solving. By knowing the causes, one can find factors that are within one's control and then change or modify them to meet one's goals and objectives. By understanding the nature of the cause and effect principle, one can build a diagram that helps to solve everyday problems every time.

The Cause-and-Effect Diagram helps to identify all the possible factors causing a specific problem. Also known as Ishikawa or Fishbone diagram, it resembles the skeleton of a fish. The problem statement is represented as the fish's head. The purpose of the cause-and-effect diagram is to identify probable causes of the problem statement summarized in the box at the fish's head.

A straight line extends out from the fish's head, or the problem statement. Diagonal lines are then connected to the straight line, each of which represents one of the major causes of the problem. Additional lines are then added to the diagonal lines, breaking the major area down into smaller areas. More lines are added until finally, at the lowest level, individual root causes of the problem are identified.

The four steps in constructing a cause-and-effect diagram are mentioned below:

1. *Determine a problem statement and categorize four or five possible causes of the problem.* Major categories of causes include policies, procedures, people, equipment, work environment, measurement, management or money. Use any category that fits the situation and helps people think creatively.
2. *Construct a cause-and-effect diagram.* Place the problem in a box on the right side of a flip-chart page and draw a horizontal line (the fish's "spine") leftward from the box.

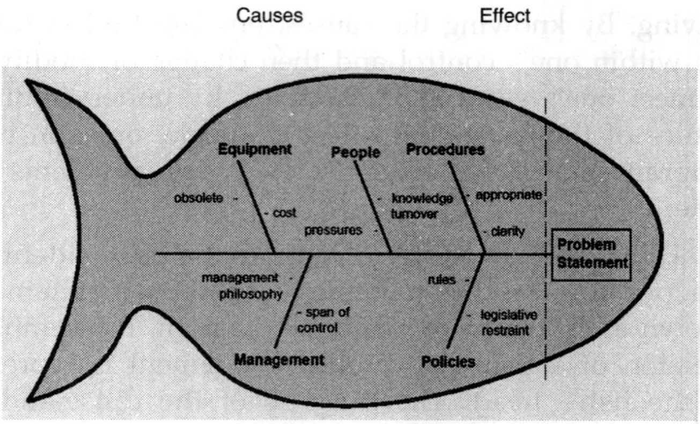

List two to three major causes in the categories above the horizontal line and a similar number below, connecting them with lines (the fish's "bones") to the "spine."

3. Conduct a brainstorming session to determine the specific factors the team believes to be causes of the problem in question; as these factors are identified, list them under their appropriate major category.
4. After all ideas are presented and understood, the group identifies the most likely causes (either by voting or group discussion). Causes, that are quantifiable, should be measured. This will provide a basis for prioritising the causes.

PARETO CHART

A Pareto chart is a vertical bar graph used to determine the most serious of a group of problems, so that priorities may be set. This analysis is based on the assumption that problems have different levels of importance, and that organizations always face more problems than their time and resources can address. Pareto analysis is responsible for the famous "80/20" doctrine, a rule of thumb that holds that about 80 per cent of the problems in any organization are created by 20 percent of its employees. The review can focus on the most vital problems by using a Pareto chart.

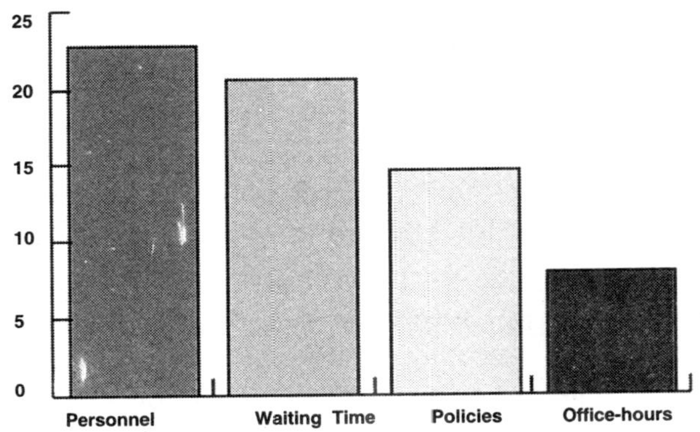

Pareto chart—Number of Complaints from January-March 2011

Suppose an organization is suspect to take too much time to issue permits. Then, it is necessary to identify problems causing this delay and correct the most significant ones. Studying the problem may indicate that the highest number of delays occur because of incorrectly completed applications. Now the review can focus on improving the accuracy of applications to resolve the most significant reason for delays. This is the sort of judgement facilitated by Pareto charting.

To construct a Pareto chart:

1. Select the issues or causes to be ranked.
2. Select a measure for comparison, typically frequency (number of occurrences) or cost. If you do not have a direct measure for a cause or problem, try using a percentage.

3. List the issues or causes from left to right on the horizontal axis in order of decreasing frequency or cost.
4. Analyse the chart and choose the most significant issues for review.

FLOW CHARTS

Flow charts are analytical tools commonly used to identify problems. They illustrate the flow of an activity, a process or a set of interrelated decisions or communications from beginning to end.

Flow charts can be applied to anything from the processing of a tax return to the flow of materials in a manufacturing process. The major benefit of flow charting is that the process forces analysts to understand all the steps of a process and to ask questions about the sequence of events in a process.

Flow charts are prepared from information gathered through interviews or observations. If an organization under review has already prepared a flow chart of an activity, verify the steps involved. Activities should be shown in sequence and significant time lapses during and between processes should be noted. It is best to use common, agreed-upon flow chart symbols so that the work will be readily recognizable to team members.

The layout of a flow chart can be either vertical or horizontal. After the chart has been drafted, its contents should be reviewed by those who provided the information involved. This review will often produce modifications to the flow chart. Once the chart's accuracy is verified, the analyst is ready to analyse the process it portrays. In this analysis, look for duplicated activities, activities that should be performed but aren't, unnecessary activities, misuse of time and any unusual occurrences.

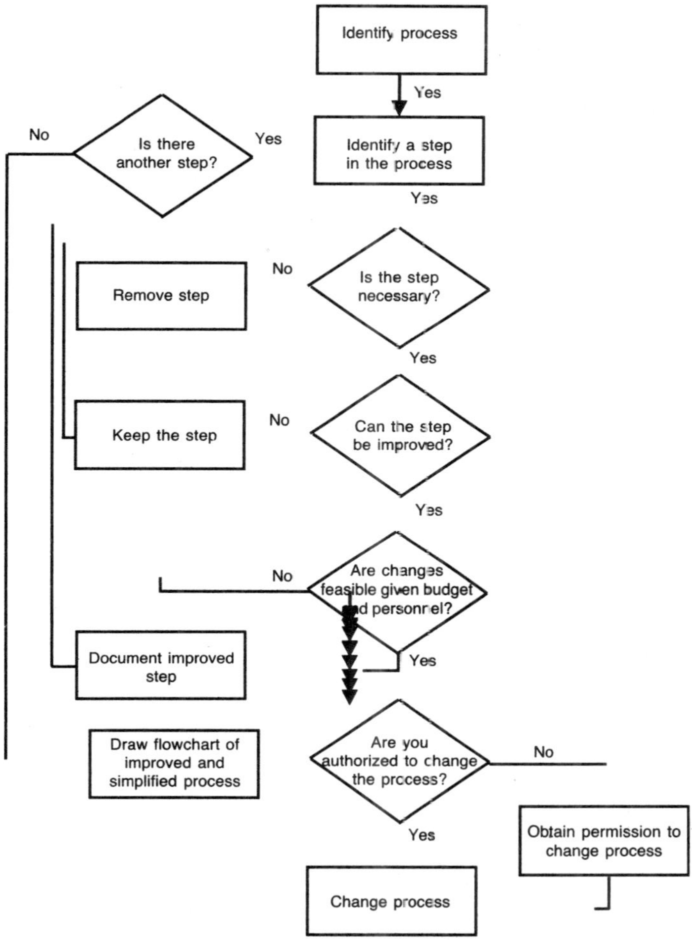

Quality Management Process Flow Chart

HISTOGRAMS

A histogram is a bar chart mainly used to show the frequency of certain activities. In a histogram, the horizontal axis signifies some quality being measured, while the vertical axis measures frequency. For example, an analyst could use a histogram to chart employee use of sick leave. To construct a histogram for this purpose:

1. Gather data.
2. Divide the data into manageable categories. The number of categories (the bars in the graph) will determine how much of a pattern will be visible. For example, appropriate categories might be zero to four days' leave used per year, five to nine days' leave per year, 10 to 14 days' leave per year and 15 or more sick days used per year.
3. Construct the histogram based on your data, with the vertical axis representing frequency, and in this case, the number of employees. The horizontal axis would represent the categories of leave used as established above.
4. Analyze the histogram to determine whether employee sick-leave patterns seem unusual or problematic.

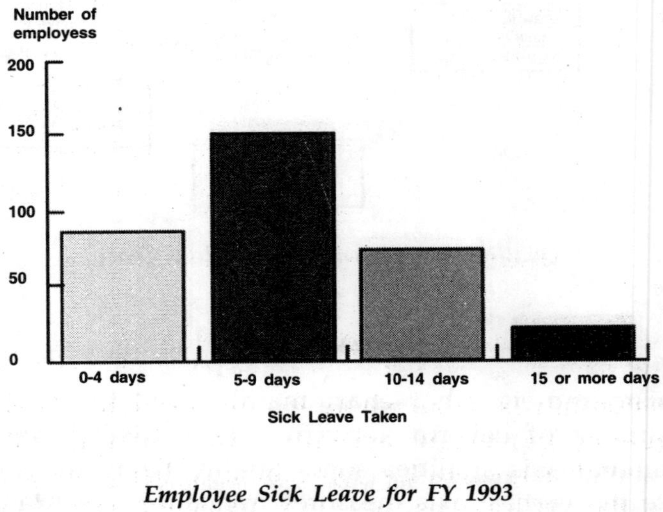

Employee Sick Leave for FY 1993

CHECK SHEET

A check sheet is used to compile, summarise and track observations, interview results or other data. It can help translate opinions into facts by showing how often an event occurs or the amount of time an activity requires.

Visually, a check sheet is simply a series of rows and columns denoting activities and categories. Creating one involves the following steps:

1. Determine the activity you wish to track.
2. Design a form that is clear and easy to use, making sure that all columns are clearly labelled, with enough space to enter the data.
3. Record the data on the form in a consistent manner.
4. Analyse the data.

Type of Complaints	Delhi	Mumbai	Kolkatta	Total
Presonnel	卌 II	卌	IIIIIIIIII	24
Policies	III	卌 III	IIII	15
Waiting Time	IIII	卌 III	卌 IIII	21
Office Hours	II	I	IIII	7
Total	16	21	28	67

Check Sheet of Complaints by Field Offices

SCATTER DIAGRAM

The scatter diagram is another tool for determining cause-and-effect relationships. A scatter diagram charts two variables on vertical and horizontal axes to determine whether there is a relationship between them—typically, whether one variable is a cause of the other.

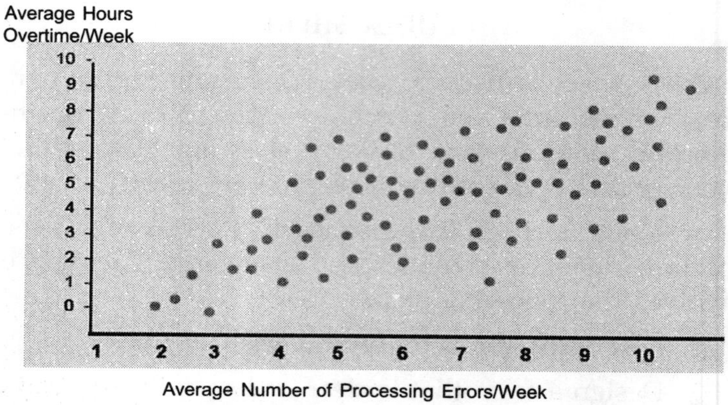

Scatter diagram—Relationship of Overtime to Processing Errors

An example of a use for the scatter diagram could be an analysis of the relationship of overtime to processing errors among workers. To create a scatter diagram:

1. *Collect the data and construct a data table.* For the example cited above, the overtime hours worked and errors made over a given time period for a selected group of employees may be assembled.
2. *Draw the horizontal and vertical axes of your diagram,* with values rising as the reader moves up and to the right. Place the possible "cause" variable on the horizontal axis (in this case, overtime worked) and the "effect" variable on the vertical axis (the number of errors made).
3. *Plot the data on the diagram. Interpret the diagram.* A cause-effect relationship is indicated if the plotted points form a clustered pattern. The direction and tightness of this cluster determines the relationship between the two variables. The more the cluster resembles a straight line, the stronger the relationship between the variables. If the cluster rises diagonally to the right, the suspected factor appears to be a cause of the problem. If the cluster

falls diagonally, the suspected cause actually appears to discourage or suppress the problem. If the data points are scattered over the whole diagram, no correlation between variables is indicated.

BRAINSTORMING

"Brainstorming" is a technique for generating useful ideas through open, freewheeling discussion among team members. Brainstorming is intended to expand available alternatives, look beyond obvious solutions, encourage innovation, shift points of view, challenge tradition, reduce inhibitions and tap the team's creative resources.

The three basic brainstorming methods include:

i) the unstructured approach in which everyone contributes ideas spontaneously, with a designated scribe or "facilitator" recording them;

ii) a structured format, in which each team member takes a turn at presenting ideas; and

iii) a written, or "pen-and-paper" method, in which participants record their ideas on slips of paper and submit them to a facilitator or team leader.

After choosing an appropriate brainstorming method, the team leader should state a problem or discussion topic. This topic or problem should be clear and concise. Place the statement on a flip chart so everyone can refer to it and then solicit ideas from the group members.

Some tips for successful brainstorming include:

i) Never criticise or evaluate an idea when it is first presented, and record all ideas;

ii) appoint a good facilitator to ensure that everyone participates and that questions that need to be asked are actually addressed;

iii) keep the setting informal;

iv) encourage offbeat and unconventional ideas;

v) combine and build on ideas, and move quickly from one member to the next.

The brainstorming session is complete when all the participants' ideas are recorded.

After all ideas are recorded, select the most fruitful alternatives, either by having participants vote for the best ideas or by reaching consensus through discussion. The top choices should be discussed in detail. Try listing each idea's advantages and disadvantages.

APC TOOL

APC stands for:

— Alternatives

— Possibilities

— Choices

The three words are close in meaning, although one or more may be more appropriate in a given situation.

Doing an APC means thinking of alternatives, or different approaches then, with these multiple choices before us, we can select what seems to be the best solution.

Generating alternatives opens up possibilities. It requires special mental effort as the human brain naturally looks for patterns and certainty rather than alternatives. That is why a thinking tool such as APC forces the mind into new directions, into actually focusing, concentrating on alternatives.

THE IDEAL SOLUTION METHOD

In this method the alternatives are listed and then

ignored. Instead, an 'ideal solution' is fashioned for the situation.

Once that is considered, the list of alternatives can be consulted again to see which one of them comes nearest to the 'ideal solution'.

So the alternatives are now considered not on their own individual merit but according to how close they come to the 'ideal'.

THE TEC FRAMEWORK

— T stands for Target

— E stands for Expand and Explore

— C stands for Contract and Conclude

This framework can be put into a time-limited 5-minute problem-solving session.

Spend 1 minute on Target and Task: The target is the precise focus of the thinking and the task is the thinking task to be performed.

Spend 2 minutes on Expand and Explore: Open up the phrase, explore the territory, pull in information and concepts.

Spend 2 minutes on Contract and Conclude: Try to make sense of when you have come to a definite conclusion or solution.

By strictly timing ourselves according to this framework the mind really focuses and produces results!

5

ART OF DECISION-MAKING

Decision-making is about deciding what action to take; it usually involves choice between options. The object of problem-solving is usually a solution, answer or conclusion. The outcome of creative thinking, by contrast, is new ideas. Any leader such as yourself who aspires to excellence obviously has a vested interest in seeing that the best decisions are taken, that problems are solved in the optimum way and that the creative ideas and innovations so necessary for tomorrow's business flow freely. Of course, everyone in the team or organization should be engaged in meeting these essential requirements. But you are the one who is called to provide the intellectual leadership that is needed.

One step towards that end that you should definitely take is to become master of the *processes of practical thinking,* the processes that lie behind all effective decision-making, problem-solving and creative thinking. You cannot guarantee *outcomes*—for luck or chance plays a part in all human affairs—but you can at least make sure that you use the well tried-and-tested processes of thinking to some purpose. You own that responsibility.

MIND AT WORK

Behind your practical, everyday thinking there lies the

most complex thing in the known universe: the human mind. Nobody hires and pays you nowadays for your physical strength. You are employed because you have a mind—and can use it effectively.

There is a vital distinction between brain and mind. Take a computer as an analogy. Your brain is what you see if you open up the back of the computer—all those chips and circuits—whereas the mind is what appears dynamically on the screen.

There are two aspects to the mind: the information it can store in the memory, and what it can do. What we call technical or professional knowledge usually involves both. You not only need knowledge about a subject but you also need to be able to apply it in a variety of unforeseen situations.

Such applications of professional knowledge invariably involve the activities of decision-making and problem-solving. A doctor, for example, is problem-solving when he or she tries to diagnose the cause of your weak left leg. Indeed, decision-making and problem-solving are so bound up with particular kinds of information or knowledge—areas of professional competence—that we find it hard to think of them in the abstract.

The physical base of your mind is of course your brain, the grey matter housed in your head. Your brain is composed of about 10,000 million cells. In fact it has more cells than there are people on the face of the earth! Each one of those cells can link up with approximately 10,000 of its neighbours, which gives you some 1 plus 800 noughts of possible combinations.

Our potential brain power is known to be far greater than the actual power it achieves. No one has remotely approached the limits of it. One estimate suggests that we use no more than about 10 per cent of our brain power.

So don't be worried by the fact that you are losing about 400 brain cells every day—indeed, if you do not exercise your mind throughout your life your brain will shrink at a faster rate.

The following three problems are not just brain-teasers: they illustrate principles about thinking

Problem 1: The Nine Dots

Take a piece of paper larger than this page and put on it a pattern of nine dots, like this:

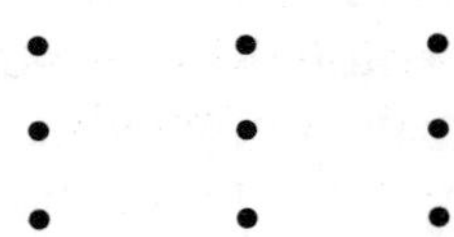

Now connect up the dots by four straight consecutive lines (that is, without taking your pen or pencil off the paper). You should be able to complete this task within three minutes.

Problem 2: The Six Matchsticks

Place six matchsticks—preferably of the wooden variety—on a flat surface. Now arrange the matchsticks in a pattern of four equilateral (*i.e.* equal-sided) triangles. You may not break the matchsticks—that is the only rule. Again, you should be able to do it within three minutes.

Problem 3: Who owns the zebra?

Having got the two easy ones safely behind you—well done if you have solved both those problems—we come now to something a little more demanding, so you must call up your reserve brain cells. The world record for solving *both* parts of this problem is 10 minutes.

1. There are five houses, each with a front door of a different colour, and inhabited by people of

different nationalities, with different pets and drinks. Each person eats a different kind of food.

2. The Australian lives in the house with the red door.
3. The Italian owns the dog.
4. Coffee is drunk in the house with the green door.
5. The Ukrainian drinks tea.
6. The house with the green door is immediately to the right (your right) of the house with the ivory door.
7. The mushroom-eater owns snails.
8. Apples are eaten in the house with the yellow door.
9. Milk is drunk in the middle house.
10. The Norwegian lives in the first house on the left.
11. The person who eats onions lives in the house next to the person with the fox.
12. Apples are eaten in the house next to the house where the horse is kept.
13. The cake-eater drinks orange juice.
14. The Japanese eats bananas.
15. The Norwegian lives next to the house with the blue door.

Now, who drinks water and who owns the zebra?

Functions of the Mind

Let's now look at how the mind works. There are three main functions: analysing, synthesizing and imagining, and valuing.

In the applied forms of effective thinking—decision-making, problem-solving, and creative or innovative thinking—all three of these functions are at work. It is their underlying health that largely determines the quality of your thought. Few people have them in harmonious balance, as shown in the illustration above. Most of us are better at one rather than the other two.

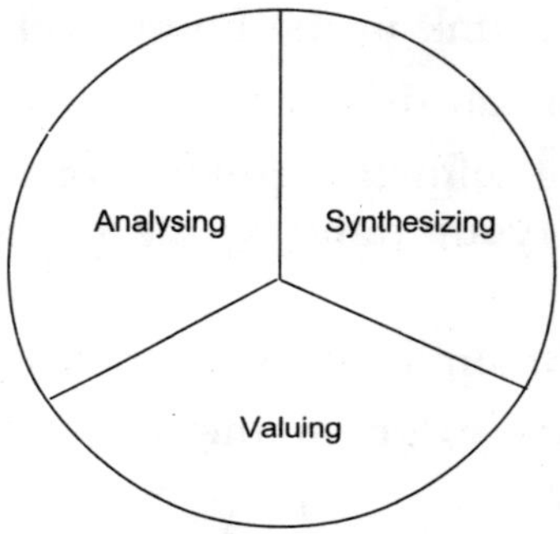

Main functions of the mind

Our differing mental strengths are a powerful reason why we need each other: effective thinking in all its forms is both a solitary and a social activity. You should always see yourself alternately as thinking alone (for yourself) and as thinking with others—either face to face or, as in this case, by reading or some other method of communication. Still, it is a good idea to seek to develop your skills in the weaker areas, like a person building up muscles in a limb through exercise: you will not always have the right people at hand to correct your bias towards a particular function.

Analysing

The word 'analyse' comes from a Greek verb meaning 'to loosen', and it means separating a whole into its constituent parts. In tackling the 'Who owns the zebra?' exercise you were using your analytical skills of dissection, trying to break down the task into its parts.

Analytical thinking is closely related to logical or step-by-step reasoning. You may have noticed that one of the skills you were using in tackling that particular problem was your power of deduction.

Logic has two main parts: *deduction* and *induction*. Deduction means literally to subtract or take away. It is the process of deducing a conclusion from what is known or assumed. More specifically, it is a question of inferring from the general to the particular. 'All swans are birds. This is a swan. Therefore...' Induction works the other way round. It is the process of inferring or verifying a general law or principle from the observation of particular instances—the core of the 'scientific method'.

Synthesizing

It is not easy to give a single label to the second function. Synthesizing—another Greek word—is putting or placing things together to make a whole. It is the reverse process of analysing. You can synthesize things with your hands, which you do whenever you assemble or make anything. All products and services are the results of syntheses. But you can also do it mentally.

When that happens, another faculty is called into play—imagination. Now, imagination works in pictures, and a picture is a whole that is more than the sum of its parts. If you shut your eyes for a moment and think of your house or your car, you see a picture. In fact, it is almost impossible not to see a picture. Your computer-like memory flashes it up on the inner screen of your mind very quickly. What you see is neither a pile of bricks, in the case of your house, nor a heap of car components, but in each case a whole.

If, so to speak, you turn up the volume knob of your imagination, you can see things that do not exist. Imagine, for example, a 56-metre-tall man... This road takes us into how to generate ideas.

The link between creativity and the synthesizing process is clear when you contemplate how nature works. A baby arrives whole and it grows. Nature is holistic. A famous South African, Field Marshal Jan Smuts, who was also a keen agricultural scientist, coined the word holism to describe nature's way of creating wholes by ordering or grouping various units together. The essential realities in nature, Smuts argued, are these irreducible wholes. If analysed into parts, they lose their essential holistic quality. As the poet William Wordsworth put it, 'We murder to dissect.' Your mind has a holistic dimension. It can think holistically—in terms of wholes—as well as analytically.

Valuing

The third function comes into play in such mental activities as establishing success criteria, evaluating, appraising performance, and judging people—as, for example, in a selection interview. Criticism is a form of valuing.

Incidentally, criticism, as commonly understood, most often suggests disapproval—some sort of a negative judgement. But in its more formal use it can suggest neutral analysis or even approving evaluation. Judgement is not always unfavourable.

In all valuing there is an objective (outside yourself) element and a subjective one. We are all born with the capacity to value. What we *actually* value—our values—depends very largely upon our environment and its culture.

Values are rather like colours. What is the colour of grass? 'Easy,' you reply. 'It is green.' But scientists tell us that grass has no intrinsic colour: it is merely reflecting light in the wave band that we call green. The structure of our eyes is also a factor. Our subjective contribution to the perception of colour is significant.

The word value comes from a market metaphor: it is what you have to give in order to receive something across the counter. The invention of money revolutionized bartering. One merit of money is that it was a universal measuring stick. But there are plenty of other values that enter into any form of decision-making, especially in business today.

CLASSIC APPROACH TO DECISION-MAKING

In decision-making there is a classic five-step approach that you should find extremely helpful. That does not mean you should follow it blindly in all situations. It is a fairly natural sequence of thought, however, and so even without the formal framework you would tend to follow this mental path. The advantage of making it conscious is that it is easier to be swiftly aware when a step is missing or—more probably—has been performed without understanding or intention.

Logically they should be played in strict sequence. But the mind darts about. The notes can be combined in different sequences and mental chords. Thinking is not a tidy process, but it should be done with a sense of order.

Remember that we are not talking here about just big decisions, for there's a lot more to running a business than making one life-or-death decision. Indeed no decision, no matter how big, is any more than a small fraction of the total outcome. Yes, some decisions are much bigger than others, and some are forks in the road. But it is really more the case that a much larger number of small decisions have a cumulative result. By hindsight we can usually identify those few pivotal decisions, but it is really the stream of smaller decisions over time, made and executed with a craftsman's skill, that yields great outcomes.

Define the Objective

Do you know what you are trying to achieve? You do need to be clear—or as clear as possible—about where you want to get to. Otherwise the whole process of decision-making is obscured in a cloud. As the proverb says, If you do not know what port you are heading for, any wind is the right wind. If you are in doubt about your aim, try writing it down. Leave it for a day or two, if time allows, and then look at it again. You may be able to see at once how it can be sharpened or focused.

Collect Relevant Information

The next skill is concerned with collecting and sifting relevant information. Some of it will be immediately apparent, but other data may be missing. It is a good principle not to make decisions in the absence of critically important information that is not immediately to hand, provided that a planned delay is acceptable. Remember the distinction between available and relevant information. One classic mistake is to look at the broad decision and then turn to the information we have that will help us decide. Some thinkers do not, however, look at the information at their disposal and ask themselves, 'Is this relevant?' Instead they wonder, 'How can I use it?'

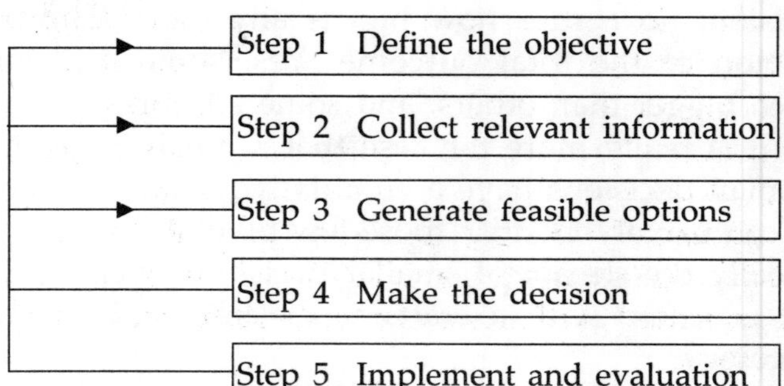

Classic approach to decision-making

Life would be much simpler if you could just use the information at your disposal, rather than that which you really need to make the decision! So often quantities of data are advanced—there are acres of it on the internet—that merely add bulk to, say, a management report without giving its recommendations any additional (metaphorical) weight.

The rapid growth of methods of communication such as faxes, voice mail, e-mail, junk mail and the internet has now contributed to a new disease: Information Overload Syndrome. A recent international survey of 1,300 managers listed the new disease's symptoms, which included a feeling of inability to cope with the incoming data as it piles up, resulting sometimes in mental stress and even physical illness requiring time off work. The survey found that such overload is a growing problem among managers—almost all of whom expect it to become worse.

Executives and their juniors say they are caught in a dilemma: everyone tells them that they should have more information so they can make better decisions, but the proliferation of sources makes it impossible to keep abreast of the data.

The growth of information has been relentless. No wonder that half the managers surveyed complained of information overload, partly caused by enormous amounts of unsolicited information. The same proportion also expected the incredible expansion of the internet to intensify the problem year-on-year.

Suppose that the overlap between information required and information available is not sufficient: what do you do? Obviously you set about obtaining more of the information required category. But getting information or—to use a grander description—doing research incurs costs in time and money. Your organization may not be in the business of making profits, but it certainly has to be business-like when it comes to containing costs.

What the graph below suggests is that you usually acquire a great deal of relevant information in a relatively short time and, possibly, at a relatively low cost in money. But the line soon curves towards a plateau. You will find yourself spending more and more time to discover less and less relevant information.

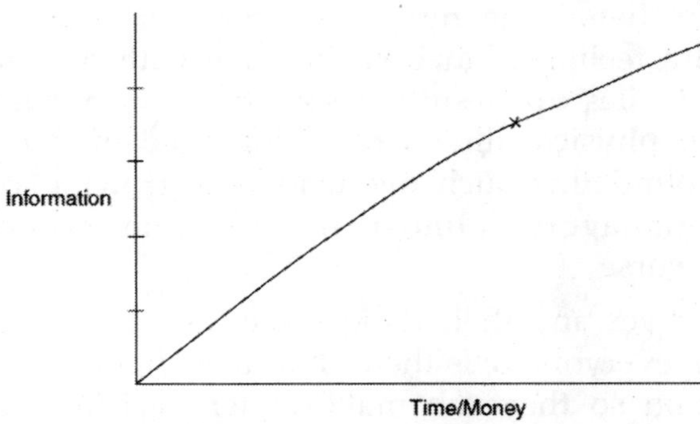

Time/information curve

Generate Feasible Options

Notice the word *options* rather than *alternatives*. An alternative is literally one of two courses open. Decision-makers who lack skill tend to jump far too quickly to the either–or alternatives. They do not give enough time and mental energy to generating at least three or four possibilities. As Bismarck used to say to his generals, 'You can be sure that if the enemy has only two courses of action open to him, he will choose the third.' Alfred Sloan, the renowned President of General Motors, was even known to adjourn meetings in which he was presented with two alternatives. 'Please go away and generate more options,' he would say. You need to open your mind into wide focus to consider all possibilities, and that is where generating ideas comes in. But then your valuing faculty must come into play in order to identify the feasible options. 'Feasible' means capable of being done or carried out or realised. If it is feasible it has some real likelihood of being workable. It can attain the end you have in mind.

Suppose you are choosing between five medium-sized estate cars for your family. It is easy to eliminate the unsuitable ones. As you work on it, for example, you may discover that one of the cars is 9 inches longer than the others, which will cause you a problem given the size of your garage. As for a second car, on studying the specifications you cannot see why it is Rs.9600 more expensive than the rest—apart from its prestigious name. So you drop that one too, leaving you now with three choices. You will notice another principle coming into play here, which (subject to the information/time curve) does take most of the pain out of decision-making.

MAKE THE DECISION

The critical preliminary activity here is to establish the selection criteria. It is worth dividing them into different levels of priority.

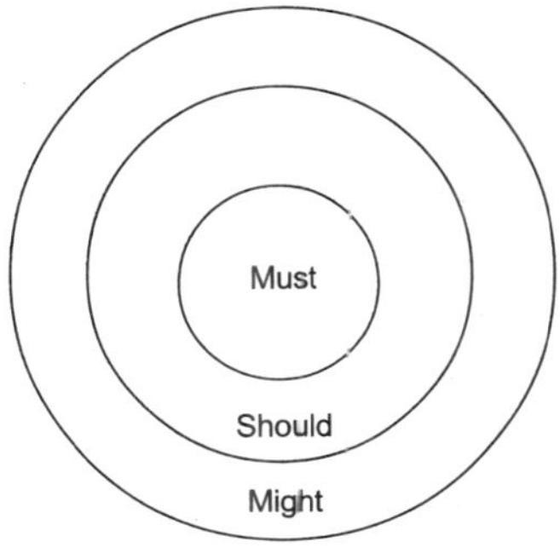

Decision-making criteria

Unless an option meets the Must requirements you should discard it. But after the essentials have been satisfied, the list of desirables—highly desirable Shoulds or pleasant addition Mights—comes into play.

Choosing a car is a relatively simple case, because there is a finite number of models to choose from and a relatively simple list of criteria. In order to help you choose in more complex cases, remember that you can make a decision by:

- listing the advantages and disadvantages;
- examining the consequences of each course;
- testing the proposed course against the yardstick of your aim or objective;
- weighing the risks against the expected gains.

RISK ASSESSMENT

What makes decisions really difficult is the factor of high risk. You may recall the conflicting advice of the two proverbs *Look before you leap* and *He who hesitates is lost.* There is an important skill in calculating risk. Calculation sounds mathematical, and there are plenty of management books with 'decision-making' in the title that offer various 'probability theories' and statistical methods to take the pain out of risk assessment. Sometimes it can help to assign numbers and calculate in that way, but the contribution of mathematics to this field is very limited. Experience plays a much larger part.

One helpful idea is to define the worst downside—what happens in the worst scenario? Can you accept that, or will it sink you? But in high-risk/high-reward situations, although you may know that you will be sunk if it does not all work out, you may still decide to take the high-risk course because the reward is just too important for you to forgo it.

You then have to address your mind to doing all you can to reduce the risk. It is here that experience, practice, consultation with specialists, reconnaissance and mental rehearsals may all be relevant techniques. You are trying to turn the *possibility* of success into the *probability* of success, but you will not be able to eliminate risk altogether: in this situation there are too many contingencies.

CONSEQUENCES

Consequences come in two forms: *manifest* and *latent.* Manifest consequences are ones that, in principle, you can foresee when you make your decision. Any reasonable person with the knowledge, experience, or skill expected of someone in your position would foresee those consequences. If you try to rob a bank, for example, the *manifest* consequences are obvious to any reasonable person:

- You might become amasingly rich.
- People, including you, might get hurt.
- You could be sent to prison.

Latent consequences are different in that they are not nearly so probable, or even possible, and a reasonable person might be forgiven for not seeing the knock-on effects that result from the complex chain of events triggered off by a decision. Admittedly, with the aid of computers it becomes a little easier in certain fields to identify latent consequences, but it is seldom possible to insulate yourself against pleasant or unpleasant surprises. We just cannot foresee the future in that way.

The emergence of *latent* consequences, of course, triggers off another round of decision-making and problem-solving activity. Yet solutions are the seeds of new problems.

Introducing performance-related pay for individuals, for example, solves some motivational problems, but what other problems does it tend to create for teams and organizations, not to mention the individuals concerned?

If we knew all the *latent* consequences of all our decisions at the time of making them, we should soon decide to stay in bed all day and never make another decision! But that decision in itself would have manifest and latent consequences... All that we can do, as humans and not angels or gods, is to make the best decisions we can, given the infirmation and circumstances, and then make other decisions to deal with the latent consequences as they arise.

Remember that there is a big difference between a wrong decision and a bad decision. A wrong decision is choosing to dig your only oil well in this place rather than that one. It's an expensive mistake, but the fault lies with the method. A bad decision is launching the space shuttle *Challenger* on a severely cold morning when the contracting engineers responsible for the seals in the engines have predicted a nearly 100 per cent chance that the seals will fail in such conditions. They did—with a tragic loss of life. Here the method or process of decision-making was deliberately ignored or irresponsibly put on one side.

The distinction is important because it separates *outcomes,* which you cannot fully control because of the part that luck or chance plays, from *process,* which you can. Wrong decisions are an inevitable aspect of life, both in our personal and professional lives. We redeem them by learning the lessons they teach us, paying the fees that life charges as cheerfully as we can. But bad decisions are predictable pitfalls; they are unforced errors.

IMPLEMENTING THE DECISION

Decision comes from a Latin verb meaning 'to cut off'. It is related to such cutting words as 'scissors' and 'incision'.

What is 'cut off' when you make a decision is the preliminary activity of thinking, especially the business of weighing up the pros and cons of the various courses of action. You now move into the action phase. Out with your cheque book—start talking about delivery dates! Things begin to happen.

It is always worth identifying what we call the Point of No Return (PNR), a term that comes from aviation. At the halfway point in crossing the Atlantic, it is easier for the pilot to continue to Paris in the event of engine trouble than to turn back to New York. The pilot has passed the PNR and he or she is committed.

In its wider sense the PNR is the point at which it costs you more in various coinages to turn back or change your mind than to continue with a decision that you now know to be an imperfect one. In most decisions you do have a little leeway before you are finally committed: you can still change your mind. Often, as in the case study of Conrad Hilton, it is your Depth Mind that double-checks your decision. It either whispers, 'Yes, I am satisfied' or begins an insidious and insistent campaign to make you at least review your decision, if not change your mind.

There is another reason for seeing implementation as a part in the decision-making process rather than the end of it. Your valuing faculty is bound to come into play at some stage in order to evaluate the decision. Did you get it right? Could you have made the decision more quickly or more gracefully, perhaps at less cost to others? All this data goes into your memory bank and informs the Depth

Mind, so that the next time you make a similar decision this information about your past may be available to you in the form of a more educated intuition. This is what constitutes what we call experience.

SHARING DECISIONS

A key issue in leadership is how far the designated leader should share decisions with others—team members or colleagues. Of course, it is also an issue for all of us—how far should we make our decisions after solitary and silent thought, or how far should we consult others?

Decision-making Aspect of Leadership

Before looking together at the decision-making aspect of leadership let me put it in context by reminding you of the generic role of *leader*—true for all fields of work and all levels of leadership.

If you look closely at matters involving leadership, there are always three elements or variables:

- the leader—qualities of personality and character;
- the situation—partly constant, partly varying;
- the group—the followers: their needs and values.

In fact, work groups are always different, just as individuals are. After coming together they soon develop a group personality. So that which works in one group may not work in another. All groups and organizations are unique.

But that is only half the truth. The other half is that work groups—like individuals—have certain needs in common. There are three areas of overlapping need which are centrally important, as illustrated in the figure below.

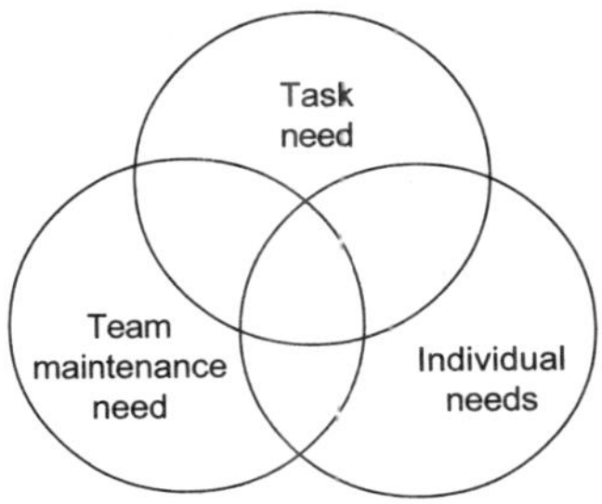

Overlapping needs

Task Need

Work groups and organizations come into being because there is a task to be done that is too big for one person. You can climb a hill or small mountain by yourself, but you cannot climb Mount Everest on your own—you need a team for that.

Why call it a need? Because pressure builds up a head of steam to accomplish the common task. People can feel very frustrated if they are prevented from doing so.

Team Maintenance Need

This is not so easy to perceive as the task need; as with an iceberg, much of the life of any group lies below the surface. The distinction that the task need concerns things and the second need involves people does not help much.

Again, it is best to think of groups that are threatened from without by forces aimed at their disintegration or from within by disruptive people or ideas. We can then see how they give priority to maintaining themselves against these external or internal pressures, sometimes showing great ingenuity in the process. Many of the written or unwritten rules of the group are designed to promote this unity and to maintain cohesiveness at all costs. Those who rock the boat or infringe group standards and corporate balance may expect reactions varying from friendly indulgence to downright anger. Instinctively a common feeling exists that 'United we stand, divided we fall', that good relationships, desirable in themselves, are also an essential means towards the shared end.

Individual Needs

Third, individuals bring into the group their own needs—not just the physical ones for food and shelter but also the psychological ones: recognition; a sense of doing something worthwhile; status; and the deeper needs to give to and receive from other people in a working situation. These individual needs are perhaps more profound that we sometimes realise. They spring from the depths of our common life as human beings. They may attract us to, or repel us from, any given group. Underlying them all is the fact that people need one another not just to survive but to achieve and develop personalty.

The Three Circles Interact

Now these three areas of need overlap and influence one another. If the common task is achieved, for example, then that tends to build the team and to satisfy personal human needs in individuals. If there is a lack of cohesiveness in the team circle—a failure of team maintenance—then clearly performance in the task area will be impaired and the satisfaction of individual members reduced. Thus, as above, we can visualise the needs present in work groups as three overlapping circles.

In whatever field you are, at whatever level of leadership—team leader, operational leader, or strategic leader—there are three things that you should always be thinking about: *task, team,* and *individual.* Leadership is essentially an other-centred activity—not a self-centred one. The three-circle model is simple but not simplistic or superficial. Keeping in mind those three primary colours, we can make an analogy with what is happening when we watch a television programme: the full-colour moving pictures are made up of dots of those three primary and three secondary colours. It is only when you stand well back from the complex moving and talking picture of life at work that you begin to see the underlying pattern of the three circles. Of course they are not always so balanced and clear as the model suggests, but they are nonetheless there.

Functions of Leadership

What has all this got to do with leadership? Simply this: in order to achieve the common task and to maintain teamwork, certain *functions* have to be performed. And a function is what you *do,* as opposed to a quality, which is an aspect of what you *are.* For example, someone has to define the objectives, make a plan, or hold the team together if it is threatened by disruptive forces.

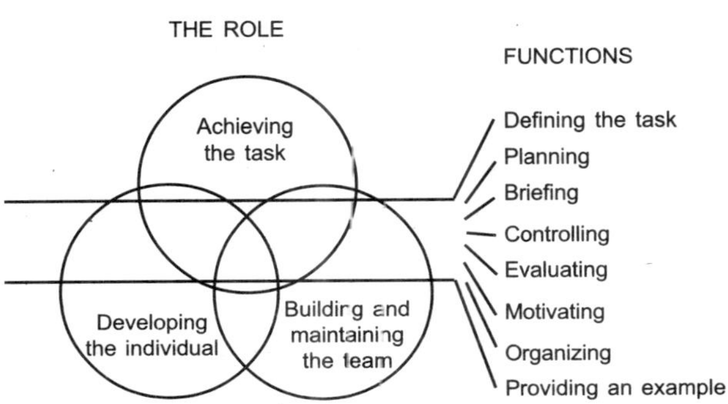

Leadership functions

Now we are on firm ground. For you can learn to provide the functions of leadership which are called for by task, team and individual needs. This is the entrance door to effective leadership. The function approach set out here is also sometimes called action-centred leadership. A function is one of a group of related actions contributing to development or maintenance, just as each part of the body has its function in relation to the whole. It comes from a Latin word meaning performance.

It should not be supposed that a leader has to perform all these functions himself or herself. Indeed, in groups of more than five people there are too many functional contributions or activities for one person to do them all on his or her own. Functions have to be shared and sometimes—in all or part—delegated. Or, putting it another way, all team members are responsible (even if not legally-speaking accountable) for the three circles. The difference between an effective team member and an effective leader is not great; it is one more of role than of commitment to all three circles or skill in meeting the common needs.

Obviously decision-making is potentially going to be an ingredient in all the functional domains. Planning is a good example. Planning means building a mental bridge from where you are now to where you want to be when you have achieved the objective before you. The function of planning meets the group's need to accomplish its task by answering the question *how*. But the 'how' question soon leads to 'When does this or that have to happen?' and 'Who does what?'

From the leadership perspective, the key issue is how far you should make the plan yourself or how far you should share the planning function with your team. Let's look at the options.

There is a lot to be said for moving as far to the right end of the continuum as you can. For the more people share in decisions that affect their working life the more they are motivated to carry them out. That consideration, however, has to be balanced against the fact that the wider you open the door of the Inn of Decision the less control you have of the outcome. The team may make a plan that, although meeting the requirements you have identified, is not the way you would have done it yourself. Can you live with that?

Just where you should act on the planning continuum depends on several key factors, notably *the time available to plan* and *the competence level of the team members*. There is no one right 'style'. The best leaders are consistent—you know where you stand with them and they are in many respects predictable. But when it comes to decision-making they are infinitely flexible. So a good leader, working with individuals or teams, will operate at different points on the scale during a day.

Once work has started on the plan, it may be necessary to revise or adapt the plan as circumstances or conditions dictate. Again, you must steer a middle course between the perennial need for flexibility as change unfolds and a certain persistence or tenacity in sticking to the agreed plan. Certainly, allowing too many unnecessary changes in the plan can itself breed confusion. As the military proverb says, *Order—counter-order—disorder.*

Always remember that everyone who works for you has 10,000 million brain cells. If time allows, it is always worthwhile to listen to people. You will be constantly surprised at the quality of the thinking and ideas available to you.

6

GENERATE IDEAS

When you are stuck in problem-solving—that is, when the techniques you have applied successfully in the past are not working—try a more creative thinking approach. You may be trying to dig the same hole deeper, worrying at your problem like a terrier, when perhaps you should be digging your hole somewhere else.

BRAINSTORMING

The best-known and most widely used creative thinking technique is brainstorming. It was introduced in the 1930s, so it has been around a long time—a sign of its usefulness. You can employ its principles when you are thinking alone, but they work better in a team setting.

When brainstorming, don't overlook the obvious! The obvious solution is sometimes the best. It may not, anyway, be obvious to everyone; and it may be possible to twist an obvious idea into something not so obvious. Don't fear repetition, either! Accusing someone of being repetitive is a form of adverse criticism and should be avoided. The same idea may trigger a different response at a different time in the brainstorming session.

Take the common paperclip as an example. In five minutes one brainstormer came up with the following new uses.

Pipe cleaner	Fuse wire
Nail cleaner	Letter opener
Tie-clip	Catapult missile
Ear de-waxer	Toothpick
Picture hook	Cufflink
Small-hole poker	Ornament
Screwdriver	Typewriter cleaner
Fishing hook	Tension reducer
Broken bra-strap mender	Zip-fastener tag mender

Guidelines for Brainstorming

- *Suspend judgement:* Give imagination the green light by with-holding the critical evaluation of ideas until later. Accept ideas without judging them.
- *Welcome free-wheeling:* Take off the brakes in your mind and go with the flow of your ideas. The more unusual the idea, the better—it is easier to tone down than think up.
- *Strive for quantity:* The greater the number of oysters, the more likely you are to find some pearls in them.
- *Combine and improve:* Listen to the ideas of others and see if you can build on them. Their way-out ideas may stimulate some buried memories or sleeping brain cells in your Depth Mind.
- *Do not edit:* Ideas should not be elaborated or defended, just quickly stated and recorded.

One major reason why brainstorming is useful is that it helps to free us from 'functional fixedness'. We have a fixed idea, for example, that a thing has only one function and that is what it is there for. By banning the use of that familiar function (in the case of scissors, the function of cutting), the mind is released to consider other possibilities. With a little adaptation, scissors would make an interesting geometrical instrument.

Take the modern British Army bayonet. Did you know that it is ingeniously designed to combine with its scabbard to form a pair of wirecutters? Or that it has a third function (officially!) built into it—that of a bottle-opener?

The essential principle behind brainstorming is simple. Please refer back to the three functions of analysing, synthesising and valuing. What brainstorming commands you to do is to make a temporary and conscious division between synthesising on the one hand and valuing on the other—for much of our valuing is negative and premature, like unseasonable frost that kills off the buds of spring. As Jean-Paul Sartre once said, 'Criticism often takes from the tree caterpillars and blossoms together.' Brainstorming's suspension of judgement is an invitation to exercise some inner mental discipline. Analysing and valuing have their time and place, but your imagination has wings—let it fly free!

How to Run a Brainstorming Session?

No more than 10 people should be involved. Some may know about the field, others may not—a mixture of both is desirable. They should ideally have been trained in the brainstorming technique before the meeting. When you run the session:

- Define the problem (using your analytical and briefing skills).
- Help people to understand the problem by highlighting the background information and history.
- Clarify the aim in a succinct sentence: 'In how many ways can we...?'

- Have a brief warm-up session, using a common problem or object.
- Brainstorm 70 ideas in 20 minutes, or a similar target. One person should write up the ideas on a flipchart. Allow time for silent reflection. Check that no critical remarks are made. Encourage cross-fertilization.
- Establish criteria for selecting the feasible ideas. Choose the best.
- Reverse brainstorm: 'In how many ways can this idea fail?'

About 40 minutes is the optimum time for a brainstorming session. But you should ask the participants to go on considering the problem and let you have further suggestions.

THINKING OUTSIDE THE BOX

Valuable though brainstorming is, not least as an introduction to one or two of the fundamental principles of creative thinking, it is not the whole story. To develop your skills as a creative problem-solver you need to adopt and practise the strategies set out below.

Brainstorming challenges one kind of unconscious assumption, namely that hammers are for knocking in nails or that scissors are for cutting. But there are other forms of unconscious assumption that may inhibit your thinking.

The reason why many people cannot do the first one is that they put an unconscious or invisible framework around the dots, and try to solve the problem within it. That is impossible. But if you break out of that self-imposed limitation, the solution to the problem is easily reached.

People assume that they must arrange the six matches in a pattern of four equilateral triangles in only one plane. If they take one small step and give themselves permission to place the matches on top of one another, they can reach the first solution. But if they break out of the two-dimensional constraint into three dimensions, they achieve the most elegant solution.

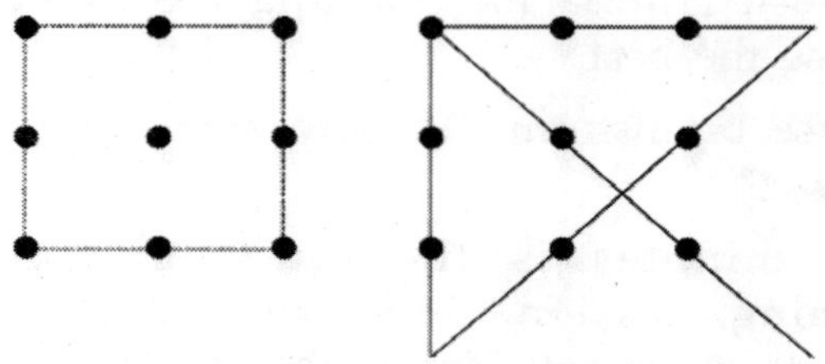

The invisible frame The solution

The nine dots' solution

Star of David Pyramid

'The six matchsticks' solution

You cannot think without *making assumptions*. But they should be conscious ones from which you can retreat when they become indefensible. The assumptions that trip you up are the unconscious ones, the constraints or limitations that you are not aware of. That is one reason why effective thinking needs social interaction. We need critical input from others to remove these filters from our eyes.

A senior manager in the marketing department of household appliance company, once had the bright idea of introducing a 'free flights' promotional scheme as an incentive for buying their products. It was a spectacularly bad decision. Some 200,000 people flew with the scheme, but it cost the company around 48 million dollars. Some 127 people sought compensation in the courts, facing Hoover with a possible bill of millions of pounds if they succeeded. The president of the company was dismissed from his post, and the owners quickly sold the company for a knock-down price. You do not get decision-making more wrong than that.

Why did this fiasco happen? Because the managers concerned made a false assumption. They assumed that when most of the people who bought appliances saw the small print wrapped about the 'free flights' offer—the complex restrictions and qualifications they deliberately built in to deter applicants—these new customers would not bother to go through such a complex approach for the sake of a free air ticket. They underestimated the public! Enough people persevered in finding a route through all the complex rules and conditions that their free flights brought the company to its knees.

This story is a parable to remind us of the importance of checking to ensure that we are not allowing unconscious assumptions to act like hidden reefs and rip the bottom of the ship.

LOOKING WIDER FOR SOLUTIONS

The phrase *thinking outside the box* ties in with the concept of lateral thinking, introduced by the well-known thinker and writer Edward de Bono in *The Five Day Course in Thinking*. Lateral thinking means abandoning the step-by-step approach and thinking, as it were, 'to one side'.

Vertical thinking	*Lateral thinking*
Chooses	Changes
Looks for what is right	Looks for what is different
One thing must follow from another	Makes deliberate jumps directly
Concentrates on relevance	Welcomes chance intrusions
Moves in the most likely directions	Explores the least likely directions

The sideways (or lateral) thinking involved often leads to reversing what appears to be the natural or logical way of doing things. For example, the earliest method of making cars involved teams of men moving from one car to another. Henry Ford turned it all upside down. He put the car frames on belts and moved them past the men—the birth of the assembly line.

It is important to think sideways because the seeds of a solution to a problem may lie outside the box you are working in. Really creative people have a wide span of relevance: they look far afield, even to remote places or times in history, for solutions to the problems they face. When the eighteenth-century agriculturalist Jethro Tull invented the seed drill he summoned up his previous experience as an organist: he was creatively transferring technology from one area to another. Most of us, however, tend to think in compartments, and the divisions in work that make specialisation possible encourage this blinkered thinking.

Always be willing to challenge widely accepted assumptions.

As the exercise 'The nine dots' and 'The six matches' illustrate, thinking outside the box means being able to spot assumptions, habits or customary ways of thinking that are widely and uncritically accepted but have no basis in reality. Many of these we breathe in by virtue of the society in which we live. They are among the everyday conventions we accept as truths without too much examination.

CREATIVE THINKING

Creative thinking cannot be forced. If you are working on a problem and getting nowhere, it is often best to leave it for a while and let your subconscious—your Depth Mind—take over. Your mind does not work by the clock, although it likes deadlines. Sometimes the answer will come to you in the middle of the night.

Grasping the principle of the Depth Mind could open the way for you to a more creative approach to problem-solving. Many people are still not even aware that their depth minds can carry out important mental functions for them, such as synthesising parts into new wholes or establishing new connections while they are engaged in other activities.

Imagine your mind to be like a personal fax machine. It would be nice and tidy if you could sit down for an hour each morning before breakfast and receive inspired fax messages from your Depth Mind. But it is not like that. The fax machine might start whirring at any time of the day or night.

If you are thinking along a certain line and nothing happens, stop. Instead of investing more time—throwing good money after bad—analyse the problem again and see if you can come up with a new approach. Usually your frustration will be caused by one of the mental roadblocks.

The processes of analysing a problem or identifying an objective are themselves means of programming the mind. Possible solutions and courses of action almost instantly begin to occur to us. Where there is a time-delay this means that the deeper parts of the brain have been summoned into action and have made what contribution they can.

How important *preparation time* is for creative thinking! Careful and clear analysis, conscious imagining or synthesising (using such techniques as brainstorming either in groups or solo), and exercising the valuing function of thought in a positive rather than negative way—all these are vital to lay the foundations for thinking creatively.

If you are planning to experiment and try a session before breakfast, it is useful always to have a preparation phase the night before. Imagine yourself as a house decorator, scraping down the woodwork and filling in holes and priming here and there, prior to painting a first coat the following day.

The Creative Thinking Process

— *Preparation:* The hard work. You have to collect and sort the relevant information, analyse the problem as thoroughly as you can, and explore possible solutions.

— *Incubation:* This is the Depth Mind phase. Mental work—analysing, synthesizing and valuing—continues on the problem in your subconscious mind. The parts of the problem separate and new combinations occur. These may involve other ingredients stored away in your memory.

— *Insight:* The 'Eureka' moment. A new idea emerges into your conscious mind, either gradually or suddenly, like a fish flashing out of the water. These moments often occur when you are not thinking about the problem but are in a relaxed frame of mind.

— *Validation:* This is where your valuing faculty comes into play. A new idea, insight, intuition, hunch or solution needs to be thoroughly tested. This is especially so if it is to form the basis for action of any kind.

Although it is useful for you to have this framework in mind, remember that the actual mental process is a lot more untidy than the above table suggests. Think of the phases as being four notes on a piano which can be played in different sequences or combined together in complex chords.

Mental Roadblocks

— *Lack of facts:* If you are not sure you have all the relevant facts, you naturally hesitate to commit yourself. Do some more research, and that may get you moving again.

— *Lack of conviction:* Maybe you find it difficult because you lack conviction in the value of this exercise or the way in which you have been asked to do it. Re-establish a worthwhile objective.

— *Lack of a starting point:* Possibly the problem seems so large that you do not know where to start. If so, make a start anywhere. You can always change it later. Inspiration comes after you have started, not before.

— *Lack of perspective:* Perhaps you are too close to the problem, especially if you have lived with it a long time or have been worrying about it incessantly. Try leaving it for a week. Consult others. Simply explaining it to them may help. They may see new angles.

— *Lack of motivation:* Do you want it to happen enough? Creative thinking requires perseverance in the face of surmountable difficulty. If you are too easily put off, it may be a sign that, deep down, you lack the necessary motivation. Reinvigorate your sense of purpose.

The function of creative thinking in problem-solving is to come up with new ideas. But remember that at some stage your valuing skills have to be brought into play. Here are six questions to ask about any new idea, solution, or course of action:

— Is it really new?

— Is it both relevant and practical?

— Whom will it involve?

— How much will it cost?

— How much will it save?

— Will it require more formal evaluation?

In times of rapid change, like our own age, there is a premium on your skills as a creative thinker. If you can think productively and constructively, as well as analytically and logically, it will give you a third dimension in all your decision-making and problem-solving.

DEVELOPING YOUR THINKING SKILLS

Winston Churchill once said, 'I am always willing to learn, but I do not like being taught.' Actually, when you learn, you *are* being taught—by yourself. No doubt Socrates, if he was here, could teach you how to think, but he is not here. Nor is decision-making and creative problem-solving a school and university subject; there is no formal body of knowledge, supported by empirical research. And so, if you truly want to develop your thinking skills, your task is essentially one of self-development.

Forming a clear picture of the kind of thinker you would like to be is the first step you need to take. A clear concept of what you might be one day can act as your magnet. Remember that point about formulating where you want to be and then working backwards?

Choode a Right Field

Thinking skills are partly generic or transferable, and partly situational. Decision-making and problem-solving are not abstracts: they are earthed in a particular field, with its knowledge, traditions, legends, and values.

Key factors in choosing your field of work

— *What are your interests?* An interest is a state of feeling to which you wish to pay particular attention. Long-standing interests—those you naturally like—make it much easier to acquire knowledge and skills.

— *What are your aptitudes?* Aptitudes are your natural abilities, what you are fitted for by disposition. In particular, an aptitude is a capacity to learn or acquire a particular skill. Your aptitude may range from being a gift or talent to simply being above average.

— *What are the relevant factors in your temperament?* Temperament is an important factor. Some people, for example, are uncomfortable in decision-making situations of stress and danger, while others thrive on them. Some prefer to be problem-solvers rather than decision-makers.

It is usually easier to identify the fields that you are not suitable for, because you lack the necessary level of interests, mental aptitude, or temperamental characteristics to do really well in them.

Design Your Learning Strategy

Before planning your own self-learning programme it is useful to remind yourself of the core process of learning.

Recall what was said above about thinking skills being partly generic and partly situational. It is when sparks jump between these two poles that learning occurs. So you need both.

Because decision-making and problem-solving are such central activities in any person's life we have plenty of experience of them. And as you move into a professional field, and begin making decisions and tackling problems, you soon build up a repertoire of experience. You learn by mistakes. In the technical aspects of your work you do have a body of knowledge—principles or theory—to bring to bear on your practice. How can you apply the same learning method to thinking skills? Here are some practical suggestions:

Put a star by the models or frameworks that you can use. Build-up your own body of theory.

- Make an inventory of your thinking skills in relation to your own field of work. What is the present profile of your strengths, and what are the areas for improvement?
- See if you can identify three outstanding decision-makers and problem-solvers in your field to whom you have access. Ask if you may interview them briefly to discover what principles—if any—have informed their own development as applied thinkers.
- Select one really bad decision made by your organization during the last 18 months. Write it up as a case study, limiting yourself to five key lessons to be learned about decision-making. If you want to develop your moral courage, send it to the chief executive!

- Now select any outstanding innovation in your field, inside your organization or outside it. By an 'innovation' I mean a new idea that has been successfully 'brought to market' as a new (or renewed) product or service. Again, write it up as a case study and highlight at the end the five or six key lessons for creative problem-solvers.
- Set yourself a book-reading programme. If you have enjoyed it, and found it worthwhile, try to read one general book each year on leadership and one biography of an outstanding person in your field. Again, underline the key principles in pencil. Surely you can budget time for one book in 52 weeks?
- Transfer your growing body of principles, examples, practical tips, sayings or quotations, and thumbnail case studies to a stiff-covered notebook. As it fills up, take it on the occasional train journey or flight and read it reflectively, relating it to your current experience.
- Take any opportunities that come your way to attend courses or seminars that offer you know-how in the general area of effective thinking. You should, for example, become thoroughly versed in what information technology can do—and not do—at present in your field, and become skilled in the use of computers.
- Lastly, go out of your way to seek criticism of yourself as a decision-maker and problem-solver. However savage, however apparently negative the criticism, you still need it in order to learn. It is the toughest part of being a self-learner, but remember the sporting adage, 'No pain, no gain.' Your critics, whatever their motives or manners, are doing you the service of true friends. Sift through their comments for the gold-dust of truth.

In any self-learning programme, experience is going to play the major part. There is no getting away from that. But if you rely *just* on learning in what has been called 'the university of experiences' you will be too old when you graduate to benefit much from the course! And the fees you will pay on the way will be extremely high.

❖❖❖

7

MAKING GOOD RELATIONSHIPS

Regardless of where they work or how long they have managed, many managers struggle to develop work relationships and communicate more effectively. Managers know the "what" and the "how" of the job. Problems erupt when communicating tasks and discussing progress. People get upset and communication breaks down. "Work would be great if it weren't for the people," many managers joke. But people problems are the predicaments that keep them awake at night So why not solve the people problems first? Perhaps it is because these challenges are both the most uncomfortable and the ones without deadlines. Or maybe it is because busy managers simply do not know how.

Topflight managers develop exceptional skills in forging relationships throughout the organization, and in particular with their own manager and direct reports. Built on trust, respect, and goodwill, a good relationship eases the exchange of information on expectations, and therefore enables successful cooperation. People more freely express their ideas when a trusting connection exists. Clarity contributes to sustaining good relationships because people learn to trust each other when they have the same understanding of roles, responsibilities, and levels of authority.

Trust, in the management context, means that you and your employees have confidence that the other person's work behaviour is consistent. Employees can rely on you for honest, direct communication of expectations. You can depend on them to get the work done as agreed because you share an understanding of what is expected. When you habitually state clear expectations, employees can tackle the assignment with conviction that they are on the right path. Knowing clearly what to do builds commitment to the work. It drives the creation and maintenance of positive working relationships.

Relationships power collegial communication of expectations and earn employee buy-in. Well-developed associations with staff are the most important key to preventing and solving communication problems. Relationships and consistently clear expectations deliver results.

POWER OF RELATIONSHIP

Good working relationships are pivotal to getting positive results and developing team harmony. When interpersonal communication at work is pleasant, people can focus on the projects and tasks instead of being sidetracked by poor relationships.

The manager's intention and decision to form good working relationships is crucial. Leaving it to chance means ignoring a great opportunity to create an environment conducive to people producing their best work.

Your staff know what your intentions are. They know whether or not you value them as persons or just as tools to get what you need done. They know if you like them or not. Managers need to communicate that they value relationships with their direct reports.

Work Relationship

Simply stated, a working relationship is a connection between people who deal with each other in some work way. The association can be required by business interactions or can be desired based on enjoyment of productively working together and trusting the other person will contribute and meet deadlines.

Relationships can be kept at the acquaintance level or can involve a continued connection that develops rapport and mutual trust. Some people may go beyond the minimum work requirements and enjoy coffee or lunch together to learn more about each other's backgrounds and interests. Others may choose friendship based on compatibility and common pursuits.

The word "relationship" intimidates some managers because they think it implies friendship or getting close to someone. They don't want to invest time in a relationship and they don't want to get personal with coworkers. In reality, it can have a minimal meaning of being respectful, friendly, and courteous and getting the work done together. It does not have to be personal.

Some managers do want to be somewhat personal but want to know where to draw the line. How personal can we be in establishing work relationships? One senior executive asked, "Most people do want to talk about their kids, but how friendly and personal can we be without being nosy?" Managers do want to play it safe and not offend direct reports. There is no one way to define work relationships. The work must get accomplished and the manager needs to create a comfortable environment with open communication so coworkers can trust and help each other. The types of relationships developed depend on the people and the situation.

Types of Relationships

Relationships vary depending upon how much both parties want to know about each other. Many neighbours have relationships. Typically they entail showing respect and meeting mutual community goals— cleanliness, safety, and regulations, if the neighbourhood has an association. Maybe neighbours collect each other's mail and papers and care for animals during vacations. One household might have neighbours they only say hello to, ones they see only at neighbourhood social functions, and others they are friends with. One size does not fit all, because there are at least two people deciding how much to interact and how much personal information to share.

It's the same thing at work. What brings people together is a task or project. Then colleagues choose how much interest to express in getting to know about where their coworkers are from, where they worked before, other places they've lived, hobbies, families, travel, and so on. And they each choose how much to tell. Despite a manager's best intentions, a particular employee may not want to discuss anything personal. Even some managers have said they don't want to disclose personal infirmation.

Work relationships don't need to be personal, but they do need to be congenial. Some managers have mentioned that they don't want to listen to direct reports' stories. But those few minutes of listening can be the bridge to employee commitment and enthusiasm about the work and the manager. Taking a little time to express interest, to show compassion when employees are sad or bereaved or ill, and to feel happiness for them when they celebrate a work achievement or personal feat can make life at the office more pleasurable and productive for everyone. Smiling, laughing, and using open body language show the manager is congenial. Setting a climate of courtesy and cooperation enables teams of coworkers to exchange their thoughts and ideas on common tasks. The better the relationships, the better the chance of collaborative results.

Relationships can make the difference in whether people want to come to work and in how willing they are to help others. A comfortable workplace invites people to be their authentic selves.

Importance of Relationships

Is there "fire" in the bellies of your coworkers? Is it passion for the work or is it sabotage? There are people who will "walk through fire" with and for us to get projects done if they like us. And, if they don't, they might "throw fire at us" to defeat our objective. Think about someone you would do almost any work for. You want to help that person meet objectives and get them done well. Why? Chances are it's because you value the relationship you share. Perhaps you want to preserve and enhance the association and the shared achievement.

You have known people on the job for whom you would "walk through fire" despite your own heavy workload and schedule. Perhaps it was taking on an extra project your boss needed done. Maybe you helped a peer who was wrestling with a tough problem. Or could it have been a direct report who needed an extra pair of hands for a crucial deadline? And you have had direct reports and peers and bosses who would work passionately to help you meet a work objective. Why? Sometimes people do the extraordinary for colleagues because it is the right thing to do or because it gets the job done. More times than not, however, it is because they value the relationship and enjoy the interaction of working together toward a goal.

On the other hand, there are some people in the workplace who are always too busy to help a coworker.

They may have personal goals, but those objectives may not be aligned with the organization. These people may not buy in to mutual goals because of their nature, personal issues, organizational obstacles, the manager, or even an experience with a previous manager. Many just do their jobs at the minimum level. Other folks will even do what they can to actively sabotage the manager's objectives. Maybe they wanted the management job. Maybe it is personal, and maybe it is just the way they behave at work. These employees are expressing fire, but not the passion of loving their jobs. The blistering behaviour seems unlikely from people who have a good relationship with their boss.

There are many reasons people don't have comfortable relationships with their managers. Sometimes it is that the manager doesn't manage the relationship, and sometimes the employee prefers not to engage. Also, some workers are extremely competent technically but don't have a natural aptitude or desire for interpersonal interactions.

Jack, a West Coast computer programmer, complained for years about management because, he said, "They don't know anything about my work but want to interfere with my decisions every now and then." Forthright, friendly communication was not part of Jack's workplace. Jack worked alone and very successfully managed a major project that didn't require much interaction with others. That's the way he liked it. Dealing with others was difficult for him because, in his words, he felt technically and intellectually superior and because he was introverted. He didn't have a relationship with his boss and he didn't want one. Any involvement of the boss was seen as interference. It was easier for Jack to blame the boss than to develop a relationship. When computer systems changed, and continual communication with coworkers or users became a requirement, he chose the "early retirement package" instead of making the transition.

Jack exemplifies some who do not want relationships and exchanges with people; they just want to do the job and be left alone. Some other people are shy about communicating. Still others are willing to learn how to work with people, but they just don't know how.

Certain people embrace conflict as just another bump in the road. Some welcome debate so that ideas can be aired and innovation can flourish. But numerous managers fear disagreement will damage a relationship or the other person will attack them or aggressively ask questions that they are unable to answer. In one class, a seminar participant said that if conflict arose in meetings at her workplace, the CEO would cover his eyes with the palms of his hands and peek out through slits in-between his fingers. That's pretty extreme body language from such a senior person, but there's no right or wrong about the fact that some people flee rather than fight. It is reality.

Adept managers frame statements in ways that do not generate conflict with coworkers. They also facilitate discussions with agility when inevitable conflicts arise. Managers need conflict radar to ensure that their employees feel free to express themselves and also feel emotionally safe. Are people really debating ideas or are they attacking each other as persons? It is in the best interest of the organization and the individuals who work there to be able to voice their ideas without being personally challenged. When the team critiques ideas against the goals instead of criticising the person, new thoughts can flourish.

A solid working relationship can make the difference in whether a person wants to come to work or not. The relationship can colour the willingness to help others. It can influence the readiness to work out misunderstandings and take mistakes in stride. Opinions and emotions about managers and coworkers vibrate strongly. Managers can take the initiative to nurture relationships and create a positive climate where employees are free to be themselves and voice their concerns without fear. When managers care about employees as human beings, they increase the possibility that employees will shape their strong emotions about work and the team into supportive excitement instead of actions that undermine the group's success.

BUILDING RELATIONSHIPS

The first step in developing and sustaining relationships at work is to decide that relationships are important in creating a productive and motivational environment. Once that value is in place, acknowledge that building relationships takes time and effort. What are some tips for forgoing work relationships? Let's look at three ways that managers communicate their intent about working with people: (1) communicating with words, silence, availability, and absence; (2) spending quality time with direct reports; and (3) creating laughing moments to lighten the environment and let people save face.

Communicating with words and silence, availability and absence

Managers communicate continually, whether or not they intend to. Everyone knows we communicate with words. But what do we communicate with silence? It might be perceived as good listening and trust or caring about the person. Or, if a trusting relationship does not exist, staff might interpret silence as a lack of knowledge or concern, arrogance, anger, or even indifference toward the work or the person. It depends upon the context, but silence communicates something.

It may not be the intended message, but employees will interpret the manager's silence through their own points of view, based on their backgrounds, experiences, and the types of relationships they have with their manager. If managers make themselves available, they communicate that the work is important and so is the person. Availability lends credibility to managerial statements that they want to help employees succeed and accomplish their goals. Many managers have told me, "I have an open-door policy, but nobody comes." Showing availability might mean putting yourself physically in neutral territory, such as walking around, hanging around the coffeepot a few extra minutes, or eating in the employee lunchroom. An employee who is hesitant to breach the proverbial open door might feel more comfortable approaching you in a casual way "out in the open" rather than behind the "open door."

If the manager is not available, again the employees interpret the absence through their own viewpoints. Such unavailability might convey trust that employees can handle the work on their own or, alternatively, be perceived as lack of involvement in the work, or it might spark other reactions similar to the responses to silence.

Spending Quality Time with Everyone

Some managers wonder how to be perceived as treating all staff fairly. One way is to spend quality time with everyone. Managers used to have a weekly one-on-one meeting with each of direct reports. These are scheduled on the same day at the same time each week so we all made the meeting a priority. We used the time to discuss progress on the project milestones, the employee's future plans on the project, expectations, and any help he might need removing obstacles or obtaining resources. One consequence of these meetings was to build and sustain relationships. We each knew what to expect and how we could work better together toward the goals.

Spending quality time with staff does not mean you have to go to lunch or socialise after work. It means everyone gets the same treatment and support for the work at hand. You and they get continual opportunist to clarify expectations and to reduce surprises on the assignments. They get regular feedback on performance toward goals in a routine meeting and thus a better chance to perform well. You each get a chance to get to know each other better.

Encouraging Laughing Moments

If it's not a safety issue, project crisis, or a major error, mistakes can be laughing moments instead of times to get hot under the collar. Most of us would rather be around a humorous person than an angry one. Emotion can be contagious and we'd rather catch laughing and happiness. If we create "laughing moments" in which we lighten up the unexpected or even mistakes, we can help people save face and realise that mistakes can contribute to learning. Laughter creates a more relaxed, pleasurable environment in which to work. It can also endear us to employees and help them use their passion to support the objectives, their managers, and their teammates. People who laugh together have more fun and a good shot at building a strong, trusting work relationship.

Enjoying Personal Relationships at Work

Even without out-loud laughing, a more personal and close relationship between workers helps create a more pleasant and effective working environment.

COMMUNICATING EXPECTATIONS

Communicating expectations is the basis for all management communication. You need to very clearly communicate unambiguous expectations to your staff. All other management functions fall into place when you lucidly communicate expectations to your team. Clear-cut expectations are the reference point for employee performance. You have to refer back to the expectations in order to deliver effective feedback and compelling coaching. Name any management function—motivating, planning, progress management, performance management, teaching, decision-making, and so on—they all depend on determining definitive requirements in the beginning.

Once you decide the course you want your direct reports to follow and tell them, you enable them to perform their duties at an acceptable or exceptional level. They cannot achieve success without knowledge of your performance expectations.

To ensure you are on firm ground when you decide expectations, you need to "manage up" and be clear on what your own boss expects of you. To be viewed as a strong leader, you must link with and be on the same page as your manager. When you communicate expectations to your staff, you must be sure that your boss is not going to change such expectations later. This would dilute your authority, slow down work progress, reduce trust, and damage relationships.

Expectations are the written and unwritten outcomes, or methods of achieving outcomes, that a manager hopes will be accomplished. The more explicitly expectations are delineated, communicated, and understood, the more likely they are to be achieved. Assumptions that a direct report knows what the manager wants delivered, or how, might end in disappointment for both parties. A decisive manager states what success should look like—either in the end result or in the method to reaching the result.

The starting points of expectations are job descriptions, performance standards, and goals. These written requirements are essential communication tools. They have great merit. Formal job descriptions and goals are, however, only the beginning of setting expectations. They are the skeletons on which skilled managers flesh out the rest of the expectations.

Many managers assume that providing written job descriptions and goals or expressing expectations verbally one time means that staff know how to proceed. If you find yourself thinking, "the employee *should know*," try substituting the words, "the employee *probably does not know*." The word *should* implies that the manager is unsure if he and the employee have the same understanding of the task at hand. Where there's lack of certainty, the employee probably does not understand the expectations to the manager's satisfaction.

Even the best employees interpret what they hear from their manager through their own experience and previous expectations of their current and prior managers. This interpretation may or may not line up with what the manager intended to say.

Many managers do not take time to crystallise their own expectations. They take the approach that they'll "know good performance when they see it" or they'll "make it up as they go along." Often these managers dole out mediocre ratings on performance appraisals because no one can measure up to a nonestablished expectation. They use phrases such as "there's always room for improvement," or "no one is perfect" as excuses to avoid awarding an outstanding rating and to distract from their inability to explain why they gave a rating that was not outstanding.

Purpose of Expectations

Managers who articulate their expectations and ensure that their direct reports understand the expectations make achieving the expectations feasible. Managers who candidly state requirements can get what they want and need: quality results delivered on time and according to budget and specification. This prevents the common miscommunications that arise when expectations are not transparent.

Consistent clarity gets the work done appropriately, with minimum errors and rework. It builds trust because the work is not a moving target. It builds relationships because employees are less stressed and they are able to succeed when they know specifically what is required. Clarity shows the decision-making and communication adeptness of a manager, and this enhances support from all directions: upper management, direct reports, and peers.

Skilled managers guide their teams to accomplish work and grow the teams to meet new demands. These managers set a clear direction that aligns with corporate vision and goals. It's the domino effect: clear expectations equal easier performance follow-up, feedback, and coaching. Once expectations are understood, managers can confidently provide the resources their team needs to produce high-quality products and services. Managers then increase the effectiveness of feedback and coaching because these functions relate explicitly to the stated expectations. So direct reports always know where they stand in relation to what the manager needs. Competent managers increase the odds of getting what they want: outstanding results, motivated employees, and a cohesive team that is happy enough to stay with the organization. For managers to get what they want, they must define exactly what the desired result will look like with turbocharged clarity. Then they need to communicate that desired outcome to the staff.

This seems so logical and yet it is not easy. Everyday there are managers who do not know how to decide on and/or communicate their expectations. This poor communication leads to decline in morale and support for management. Let's look at two examples of how lack of clear direction (1) keeps managers from getting what they want and (2) teaches employees that to survive, they must disregard their manager.

Impact of Not Setting Clear Expectations

Not being clear about the expectations costs the organization time, money, relationships, and quality results. It costs the manager her reputation and sometimes her job. Two true stories of the loss of employees' productivity and commitment, due to lack of clear expectations, follow. These are the stories of Tom and Kristen. In Tom's case, his manager cannot set expectations. This causes rework and last-minute scrambling to complete projects. In Kristen's case, her manager doesn't set expectations at first, rather only when she observes behaviour she doesn't like. Expectations after the fact come across as punitive. In both cases, work relationships and communication are strained and stressful.

Tom, an engineer, works for a consulting firm and is an expert in both construction management and claims resolution for construction disputes. Think bridges, tunnels, hospitals, airports, radioactive site re-mediation, power plants, highways, and public transportation. His work affects safety, so Tom's projects should be well planned in advance and in concert with management. Yet, for two years, Tom struggled to get direction from his boss on how to proceed on a multibillion-dollar project. Fifty per cent of Tom's time was allocated to this project.

Tom's manager insisted that they work in the same office site, yet despite the proximity, the manager was not able to provide the guidance needed to get the job done. Tom would ask his boss for direction and get no answers. His manager could not explain the expectations. So Tom did his best with what he imagined he was supposed to do. He mapped out proposed plans and recommendations for the client and submitted them to his manager to see if he was on target. The boss would act as if he were grateful, then leave the documents in a pile on his desk—where they stayed. No amount of leverage could budge the manager to make a decision on the direction of the work. There was always something else that took priority. People began to show up late for work because the work didn't seem to matter.

Since the manager did not perform the day-to-day operational work, decisions became last-minute crises. It turned out that crisis was the environment in which the manager thrived. The manager stepped out in front as soon as deadlines loomed, but the team grew frazzled. He dictated orders and the work got done on time at his employees' expense. What a waste of talented engineers' intellects, client money, and time that could have been paced properly to develop the highest quality work. Eventually, the boss was fired, but team trust, loyalty, and morale had already eroded.

Do you know people like Tom who face this uncertainty at work? Have you ever had a manager who kept you guessing? Unfortunately, Tom's experience is not unique. Many people, even managers, go to work every day not knowing what is expected. They have a general idea of what to do, so there is activity. But often they don't know what the manager's performance expectation is and therefore cannot excel in the manager's eyes. They take the blame for lackluster performance even though the manager was responsible by not articulating the desired performance. Managers cannot get what they want if they cannot identify it in specific terms.

Tom's example involved a manager who ignored both his staff and opportunities to set and clarify expectations. In the second example, we look at Kristen and her manager. This manager also does not set expectations up front. Unlike Tom's boss, who ignores the employees, Kristen's manager seeks "teaching moments" whenever she sees something she doesn't like. She explains her expectations only after something goes wrong.

Imagine people keeping a low profile and staying below the radar. You have seen them do this to prevent getting "dinged" by their manager. Managers who do not specify what they expect up front are often the same managers who nitpick the negatives later rather than focus on the whole performance picture.

POWER OF TRUST

Working relationships are built on trust. Trust establishes the framework for delegating, giving feedback, and coaching, because if people think you have their best interests at heart and you know what you are doing, they will put themselves out to help the team succeed.

Trust is the result of consistent, respectful, and factual interaction. A manager who is precise about expectations and who helps employees achieve those desired results earns trust. People want to know that their task is not a moving target and that their boss is upfront about their progress toward meeting the goal.

When trust exists, a manager can assign work and converse regularly with direct reports about performance with greater comfort. Regular feedback and listening helps everyone to know whether work should continue on the current path or be redirected. Discussing task and project status becomes an opportunity for growth for all parties as well as for enhancing the work and the relationship.

Responsibilities and Levels of Authority

Upper management support is key to helping managers develop trusting relationships with their employees. When employees know that the expectations are clear and that their manager has upper management support, it is easier for them to follow their manager and do what is asked. When their manager is aligned with organizational direction, employees can trust that the expectations will be realistic. It is less stressful for everyone because the tasks most likely will be stable. Assignments that change frequently create stress and distrust and therefore undermine a manager's *personal* power. Stable tasks enable employees to believe that the manager knows the direction and is there to support the employees achieve the goals.

In short, to set clear expectations for others, you must first know clearly *what is expected of you*. Looking at your managerial role from the points of view of your boss, staff, peers, and upper management will help you feel confident about the breadth of your scope and the extent of your authority. This 360-degree look at your responsibilities illuminates what others need from you. Used well, this knowledge can prevent misunderstandings and translate into achieving results through positive working relationships. Transparent understanding of your entire suite of responsibilities—written and unwritten—can result in gaining support from all directions and levels of the organization. It also points you to a bigger picture of where to contribute to others in supporting corporate goals.

Using a recommended worksheet will help you to communicate in a logical manner with your boss. It is critical for your success that you comprehend your roles as your boss and others see them. To effectively lead and manage your group, you and your manager must agree on your responsibilities and depth of authority. Once you solidify what your manager expects and what level of authority you have for each project or task, you can confidently delegate to and follow up with your staff. If you live in the dark, your staff will too, and they will not see you as their leader.

Expectations are frequently unwritten and often unspoken or undefined. Yet you will be evaluated on these unwritten expectations. It is your job to take the initiative to clarify your manager's expectations so you can succeed.

Many managers ask, "Shouldn't this conversation be initiated by my boss?"

"Has it?" I ask.

"No," they reply.

"Well then?" I ask.

"Point taken," they say.

Request a meeting with your boss in upper management and thoroughly prepare for it. This is a chance to show your strengths in organization and planning as well as your desire to partner with your manager.

Communicating with your manager about what he expects of you is an ongoing process. First you analyse what you think he expects. Then you meet with him to discuss these responsibilities and levels of authority. It may take more than one meeting for you to both agree. After meeting, you must continually dialogue with your manager to be sure you are on target and to include changes as they occur.

Depending upon how collaborative your relationship with your boss is and how he deals with written information, you might decide to e-mail your completed worksheet ahead of the meeting. This gives your boss an opportunity to think about his expectations, whether he agrees with what you've written, and what to add, delete, or modify. With both people prepared for the meeting, you might have better results in a shorter period of time. However, if you think your boss will e-mail it right back to you with a pithy note to avoid a face-to-face meeting, you may not want to e-mail it. For the ideal communication, you should persuade him to review it ahead of time and meet in person to discuss his expectations.

STATING PERFORMANCE EXPECTATIONS

Even unwritten expectations need to be decided upon in a specific way and then communicated, because employees cannot meet vague, unspecified requirements. If a manager instructs employees about the standard after they have erred, it is punishing and damaging to the relationship. It provokes fear in employees of making more mistakes because they don't know the rules.

Every day managers make assumptions that employees are like them or know what to do. When the employee doesn't deliver on the assumption, many managers get upset and/or blame the employee, or label him with a word like "slacker," or say he has a poor work ethic. Often it is just a misunderstanding that could easily be handled as a one-off instead of lumped under a pile of transgressions and used as an excuse to label someone. Managers make mistakes when they make assumptions. They can fix these mistakes. When managers are surprised by behaviour or lack of action, it is an opportunity to acknowledge to themselves that they need to take time to delineate what they expect and communicate it.

Guidelines and expectations are beneficial to people. Being supportive actually means letting people know the boundaries and expectations ahead of time. It is not supportive to avoid defining expectations and then watch people make unnecessary mistakes. When you tell them your expectations after they have erred, it comes across negatively and can create tension and defensiveness.

We do not do anyone any favours by not getting clear on our daily expectations. If managers don't spend the time to think about expectations ahead of time and ensure they are stated and clearly understood, performance cannot soar. Relationships get injured. Trust declines. Resentment and tension escalate.

After managers recognise their precise expectations or standards, these are set in motion by how the managers state the expectations. A managers success depends on how advanced his influence and persuasion skills are. Employees in today's workforce expect to have a say and to be heard. Most want to be told why the work is important and why it has to be done certain ways. They want to see the benefits to themselves as well as to the organization. Recognising such benefits focuses the work and enlivens it with meaning. Today's employees expect to be treated as colleagues and want to work shoulder to shoulder with their manager.

The belief that "it's their job, they don't need to know why" is not practical thinking. Management responsibility is about communication, which is how we say things. If people feel they are choosing, they feel more in control of the work. Even if there is a nonnegotiable way that a project is expected to be done, managers can explain the benefits to the employees of doing it that way. Explain how it helps them successfully reach the goals so the conversation can be viewed as supportive and collegial rather than as "bossy." Use your intuition about tone of voice and word choice. How would you like to be treated?

Managers know they are supposed to motivate direct reports or at least provide a motivational environment. That's what influence and persuasion is about—providing motivation. Strong managers persuade people to be committed to deadlines and a high level of quality. Telling people why their participation is important is an essential part of maintaining relationships and getting quality work done. Managers can get compliance in the short run with or without a good relationship, but they might get sabotaged in the long run. If people are not allowed to express their opinions or if a relationship is not valued, a manager may get what he wants done right now but lose collaboration in the future. Collaboration occurs when people work together to try to meet the needs and best possible outcomes for all parties. This benefits quality and productivity.

The way managers communicate expectations can motivate or de-motivate as an unintended consequence. Management communication skills are key to stimulating top performance. How well the work gets done is dependent on the staff. How well they work together to align personal interests with corporate interests is dependent on the manager.

What are your expectations? If you were to ask your direct reports to tell you their understanding of your expectations, what would they say? Would their understanding be the same as what *you* think the expectations are? What are the unwritten expectations many employees have to discover and wrestle with by themselves?

Typically, a manager is keenly aware and careful when discussing performance essentials during hiring interviews, new employee orientation, role and responsibility clarification, job description review and revision, and goal setting. But, more often, expectations are mentioned in passing. Managers may not even realise that they are setting expectations. As a result they don't take the time to be deliberate and think carefully about the best way to set and communicate everyday job needs.

Management activities such as work assignments and follow-up, delegation, process and project management discussions, weekly progress meetings, giving feedback, and coaching demand thoughtful consideration and consistency in message. It is also important to use paraphrasing and to ask employees to explain their perception of the expectation so you can be sure you have the same understanding.

Use your intuition about how to state expectations based on your knowledge of the work, the relationship you share with the direct report, and what the situation requires. Trust yourself. If you are prepared from the business side and you have a good working relationship with the direct report, you will know how to phrase the expectations.

When stating expectations, it is essential to tell the individual whether or not she has discretion in how to do the task. Whenever the how can be delegated, greater ownership of the task ensues. But sometimes, there is only one way to do the task because of policy, procedure, regulation, or communication needs of groups. It there is only one way to do the task, be clear about it. Following are two scenarios with suggested steps to follow and an example of each. The first scenario applies when there is a required way to do the task and the second scenario is for when the employee can decide how to do the task. When there is only one way, you tell the employee both what you except her to do and how.

When stating performance expectations, deciding how much to say and how to say it fluctuates. The amount of detail and way to talk to your direct report depends largely on the task, the delegatee, and the process. How much elasticity does the task offer for determining how to accomplish it? What is the experience and track record of the delegatee on this or similar projects? What is the grade or rank of the position the delegatee holds in the organization? How much required process or structure must be incorporated in getting this assignment done? Is the delegatee familiar with the process? Other variance factors include your company's or the customer's budget, the financial health of your company, and/or the general economy. Other crucial considerations are the time window for accomplishing the task as well as the flexibility or rigidity of the deadlines.

PROBLEMS ARISING FROM UNMET EXPECTATIONS

There are several organization-wide communication issues. These communication problems aere identified only when staff members notice that their expectations are not met. In other words, staff members did not state the expectations they had of other departments ahead of time. They expected certain actions of those groups or managers that did not occur. Instead of initiating conversations with others to clarify mutual expectations, they made assumptions. These assumptions led to disappointments now cited as communication problems.

Each of the six generic organizational communication problems includes a bulleted list of specific problems the leaders mentioned. Since these issues are common to many organizations, suggested solutions are also listed.

Problem 1. Lack of Clarity in Delivering Information

— Not communicating clearly enough with information so other groups can understand.

— Not giving a specific deliverable date.

— Not being clear on what action should be taken.
— Assuming the information is clear to others.
— Not giving consistent information.
— Giving incorrect information.

Solution: ***Deliver Clear Information***

It's important to verify the facts before delivering information. Always state the information as briefly and simply as possible. Then ask your direct reports to restate what they think they heard you say. Then ask them what they think it means to them. Ask them what action they plan to take. If you disagree on the action, discuss it right away—don't avoid it. Ask them to e-mail you their written understanding. If it's different from yours, talk (don't e-mail) to them again. Avoid "hallway delegation."

Problem 2. Management Priorities Need Clarification

— Individuals' priorities are in conflict.
— There are different objectives from group to group.
— People don't see the big picture—they're focused on their own jobs.

Solution: *Resolve Conflicting Management Priorities*

Review the priorities of all your team members to ensure that individuals' priorities are not in conflict with each other. Change any conflicting priorities by ranking tasks and projects in the order of importance to the organization. Consider the impact on organizational as well as group goals, customers, costs, launch dates, deadlines, employees, inventory, shipping, and financial health of the organization. When there are different objectives group to group, tell your boss about the effect this has on your group's progress. Unless there are political ramifications that your boss tells you about, talk to peer managers to see what you can work out together. If you and peer managers have incompatible objectives, create a mutual proposal recommending how the objectives could be aligned. Keep working with your boss and negotiate with the necessary approvers to get the priorities in sync. Your manager may have to work with higher management depending on the scope.

To help your staff see the big picture and prevent them from focusing only on their own jobs, continually talk about how each person's contribution relates to the team, and how that relates to the organizational goals. Don't assume they remember this. To show that their work is relevant to the whole, keep mentioning how.

Problem 3. Organizational Obstacles

- Physical location of team members is an obstacle. There are communication challenges due to the layout of the building.
- There is no unified information system.
- There are too many forms that don't all work together.
- People do not know what other people are doing.
- There are inconsistent or absent work orders.
- Cross-departmental chain of command isn't clear.
- File management systems are lacking.

Solution: ***Remove Organizational Obstacles***

If you do not have authority over the obstacles, research the facts on all sides of the issue, come up with potential solutions, and discuss with your boss. Persuade your manager with facts about cost, the bearing on performance and morale, and the benefits of changing the way things are currently done. Keep your staff informed about what is being done or not done regarding these organizational issues and why. Let them vent. Lead them to voice opinions about how to improve their work situation given the reality of organizational constraints.

When you do not have control over the issue, work with others who do. Make recommendations and persuade them to take action. Define what obstacles stand in the way of your team's performance. Is it the layout of the offices? In the case of one client, there were offices on both ends of a large plant where the final products were constructed and prepared for shipping. The long walk inhibited people who would have benefited by face-to-face communication with other groups across the warehouse. An expensive solution would be redoing the physical layout. A middle-of-the-road solution would be swapping offices so that interdependent groups, which interact the most with each other, would have offices on the same end of the building. The easiest, least-disruptive, and least-expensive investment would be to leave all offices alone and buy bicycles, scooters, or golf carts so people could travel quickly from one set of offices to the group on the other side of the plant. What solution is appropriate for your office is up to you. The point is to thoroughly investigate the facts of the problem and compare the costs of doing nothing to alternative solutions.

If the lack of a unified information system is hindering the work, recommend that the appropriate group research the need and options for a unified information system. Be sure they coordinate with other groups during the research as well as with senior management.

When people complain that there are too many forms and the forms don't always coordinate, determine the purpose of each form and exactly how all the forms do or don't work together. This is a study of process and workflow. What information is truly necessary to convey to whom on a task or project? Forms are meant to be communication aids, not obstacles. Who needs what information and when? Can some forms be eliminated or revised to be simpler? Are there similar forms that could be converted to one form that would travel from group to group? What are the time constraints of delivering information? What forms can be eliminated or put online?

If there are inconsistent or absent work orders, what can a manager do? This relates to process and workflow. If there are inconsistent and absent work orders, why? How many people or groups are not completing the work orders? What is the effect? If there are ineffective forms or procedures, get clear facts from direct reports on why they think the process could be improved and what they recommend. Then work with the appropriate managers whose groups are touched by the flow of the work orders and procedures. If needed, get senior management approval for any major changes in process and workflow.

If you do have control over the organizational issues, remove the obstacles. You probably have authority to resolve the last two obstacles on the list.

Clarify the chain of command across departments. It is essential that managers look into who is responsible for what part of a project—for flow of information and/or materials. Who has the authority as interdepartmental interaction is needed? If there is no authority, what are the best influencing strategies, and do your direct reports need training on getting results without authority?

Create a file management system for your group. Can you determine what the needs are or delegate the research to a direct report? What would be the simplest, least-expensive, and most-accessible file management options? What are the benefits and constraints for each alternative? Who else needs to be part of deciding if a new file management system is necessary and what would be the best choice?

Problem 4. Management Timing

- There is slow response to requests and inquiries.
- There is a lack of timely information.
- There is too little help that is too late to be useful when it is finally given.

Solution: ***Demonstrate the Importance of Timing***

Give a quick response to requests and inquiries from direct reports so they can stay on schedule. When they thank you, reinforce the value of fast turnaround with a comment about how you also value quick turnaround from colleagues.

If the lack of quick response is from other managers or groups, be like an octopus with eight legs stretching out to other managers and upper management to collaborate on solving this issue. If there is slow response to requests and inquiries or lack of timely information, meet with the appropriate peer manager and explain the situation and how it affects your group and the mutual goal you share. What is that manager's point of view on the problem? Develop a timeline together and give/get commitment to established timelines.

Problem 5. Management Lack of Follow-Up

- Managers do not check employee progress.
- Employees doubt the importance of assignments and deadlines.
- Employees are reluctant to approach manager for guidance.

Solution: ***Follow Up on Project Progress***

This management action influences much of a manager's credibility with staff. If a manager follows up, it is a statement that the work assignment and the deadline are important. This leads to being able to trust that the next assignment will be significant, not just another flurry of activity with no follow-up. With follow-up, a manager can be viewed as consistent, organised, and trustworthy. In addition, people are more likely to ask questions of their managers when their managers approach them about progress on an assignment. This helps keep a project on track.

Problem 6. General Communication Issues Throughout the Organization

- There is a lack of communication in terms of sharing project information.
- People often say, "I have a better way" rather than collaborating.
- There are trust issues.
- There are personality blocks.

Hidden behind or underlying these complaints are informal and unwritten expectations that people have of one another at work. They expect clear communication and are unhappy when it is not achieved. Teams of leaders and managers up to C-suite in one company made the above observations. But they are universal dilemmas. And they can be handled with the intention to be great communicators.

Solution: Examine General Communication Issues Throughout the Organization

Lack of communication in terms of sharing project information will improve when the organizational obstacles are resolved. Perhaps implementing a companywide online project management system would help. This is worth investigating in terms of needs, cost, time, payback, and staff time compared to what the cost is of not doing it.

If people say, "I have a better way," ask yourself, why? Do organizational obstacles such as forms and workflow create it because of the confusion? What are the ideas for a better way? Perhaps create a method for opinions to be aired, such as an invitation to submit ideas in writing when an organizational issue is going to be examined and a change might result.

Trust issues will improve when interdepartmental processes and conflicting priorities are discussed and peer managers work together toward common goals. Each individual manager must still work on open communication and relationship building.

When staff members mention that personality blocks are interfering with their work, it is an opportunity to increase understanding of and communication with others. Every workplace has a diverse array of personality types with behavioural preferences in terms of how they deal with data and people. Human Resources can help with behavioural style assessments. Participants score their answers to behavioural assessments and recognise how varied people are in terms of thinking, analysing, taking care of other people's interests, and taking action.

Many times differences and lack of communication between people are suddenly explained in a logical way. Managers can choose to flex their own style in order to work better with people who act in a different style. Work with your Human Resources department to identify an assessment and an approved way of using one in your group if you want the group members to understand each other better and to behave with greater understanding toward each other.

Ideally, clarifying expectations and working together across the organization should be handled at the top echelon of the organization. But realistically, attempts to resolve issues at other levels may preclude the information from getting to top management. Grassroots efforts are every manager's responsibility. Each manager needs to be responsible for listening to and resolving organizational and communication issues as much as possible. This starts with preventing problems in the first place by keeping direct reports informed with clear expectations and information about why their tasks and projects are important.

❖❖❖

8

SOLVING COMMUNICATION PROBLEMS

Work relationships (emotion, trust, intuition) and process (facts, steps, logic) partner to amplify effective communication. At first blush they may seem diametrically opposed concepts. But they are inextricably linked if you want your communication skills to top the charts. You must pair relationship and process to be the ultimate communicator. Sometimes a nonbusiness analogy helps clarify the point. Everyone can relate to math and theater. Let's look at how one author paired fact (mathematics) with emotion (theater).

Danielle Carroll united these two in her master's thesis, "Performances of Truth in Theatre and Mathematics". Carroll writes:

> With math set up as purveyor of fact and empirical truth and theatre positioned oppositionally in the realm of fiction and emotion, the decidedly irrational, these two systems occupy very different spheres in academic discourse. However, by placing theatrical performance and mathematics in dialogue with one another, I find that the two are more similar than I had previously thought.

Putting relationships and process "in dialogue with one another" lifts communication to a more enlightened level. Pairing these two broadens and deepens our experience both with the person and with the process. People who separate relationship from the work process often have distant, stilted work conversations. An employee working with a manager who does not blend relationship and process might be uncomfortable asking questions or admitting he is unclear about an assignment. This can lead to work performance or people problems later on. But integrating relationship and process can prevent and solve problems more quickly and satisfactorily for both parties and lead to collaborative goal attainment.

Carroll also asserts:

> Even parts of mathematics, a discipline known for its systematic nature, must be intuited. Once, in a sophomore-level math class, I approached a professor about how to create a system that could tackle all of the problems that we were doing. He responded, "there is no system. You just have to feel it out." I recall feeling abandoned; after all, I had begun my study of mathematics for its structure and certainty. Since then, however, I have learned to enjoy letting go, occasionally finding the answers to problems by accident or I suppose acknowledging that they find me. In order to discover truth, one must carve out a space in structure and system for intuition.

So it is with process and relationships. You have to "feel them out." We may want certainty, but that does not exist with either relationship or process. Both grow and change shape. One informs the other.

ROLE OF INTUITION

Processes support the search for better relationships, and relationships support the quest for better processes.

Effective managers focus on both, letting one give information about the other. Intuition springs from this information. Confident managers trust their intuition. They listen and clarify the other person's meaning, and also intuit the person as both a professional and a human being. They use intuition to frame their speech on the listener's level of expertise and interest. They also use intuition to knit together relationships and structure to make it easier for direct reports to do their best work.

WORKFLOW MANAGEMENT

A workflow process helps communication because it has a set number of steps. Everybody knows what the steps are. Within each step of a process there may be some flexibility, but everybody still knows the goal of each step.

What about project management (PM)? The same rules apply. The only difference is that the steps are not for an ongoing workflow process, but for a one-off project. The business of sales is a process. Opening a new sales office is a project. Both require a series of steps.

Getting the Work Done

Process and project management frame the work in business terms understandable to direct reports, peers, and upper management. They also facilitate setting expectations, monitoring progress, giving feedback, and coaching. Everyone knows the original plan and can compare it to the actual performance. The vocabulary is common to all and is work related rather than subjective and judgemental. When expectations are documented, information can be dispersed consistently.

Most jobs have a process, or methodology, which is a logical arrangement of tasks leading to achieving an end result. This is true for sales, engineering, manufacturing, finance, scientific fields, and IT, although the processes differ from discipline to discipline.

In fact, most managers are promoted because they are expert at the technical process demanded by their job function. As managers, they are then expected to oversee the processes and coach others to become proficient in the job process. Ironically, their managerial work will no longer be evaluated on their own outstanding process skills but on how well they communicate, work with people, and help their direct reports deliver results. Success in these responsibilities is achieved through process and relationships.

Everybody has process skills. They may be formal or informal. Using yours in day-to-day communication produces wonderful results because it gets everyone on the same page.

Process and Communication

What do process skills have to do with communication? How can process be applied to working with people? What has project management to do with preventing and solving interpersonal issues?

When people talk to each other, they often embed emotion into the conversation. Tempers can flare based on past experiences with a particular coworker or issue. When people don't get what they want, they may or may not take the time to clarify each other's meaning and work it out. One might say, "I can't believe you thought...." Or they might just jump to, "That's not at all what I meant." Yet in reality, setting and gaining understanding on managerial expectations is just business. And the more process we build into setting and clarifying the expectations, the less personal it feels to everybody. Documented process helps clarify expectations upfront, saves time, and prevents disagreements later on.

Process is systematic and logical so it is easily learned. In fact, since most folks use process in their technical areas, they can transfer that skill to dealing with coworkers. Just change the content from technical to interpersonal relations.

Handling the interpersonal aspects of the job requires blending relationship, intuition, and process. Since process focuses on using observable facts to prevent, determine, and solve problems, process is a reliable pivot point when dealing with performance issues. Referring to process can help neutralise potentially difficult conversations.

Some companies have formal processes, especially for engineering or manufacturing. Standardized process is helpful because the regular patterns make it easier for people to repeat the process next time. It saves time negotiating the way teams solve future problems or make decisions. Process provides common vocabulary and promotes clear communication because all team members use the same methodology and know what to expect and how to proceed.

Lack of process and project management can cause organizational communication problems and confusion about priorities. Sometimes lack of structure promotes miscommunication among senior management, which ripples down to the rest of the company. It can create "camps" within the company. For example, in a small company growing larger in products, revenue, locations, and staff, the CEO and president disagreed on certain strategic directions. Some departments lined up behind the CEO and others behind the president. Much of this taking sides was based on previously developed relationships. When the company was small, things got done because relationships were leveraged and there was smaller scope to agree or disagree on. Now that the company was expanding rapidly, naturally it was more difficult to stay united. More structure was now required.

These same phenomena can occur on a department or team level as well. Often managers are surprised by communication problems that erupt as growth occurs. One seminar participant said, "When our group was smaller, we just knew what the other person needed and when and we provided it. And vice versa. Things just flowed. Now we have a lot of new people and they don't get it. They don't know how we get things done." For better or for worse, the more the growth, the more the need for structure to solidify communication and thus reach the objectives. New people do not have the background or intuition to know what the team needs and how people previously operated together. They do not have the history of relationship nor the informal process that took place.

Project Management

Project management includes identifying project stages in the development cycle, estimating how long tasks typically take, and initiating a formal scheduling system that can easily be modified as multiple projects are managed across departments or functions. The system should have the capability to track accountability for meeting task deadlines. Accountability develops people and clarifies who is responsible for what.

What are the benefits of using project management? It reinforces communication about who is responsible for what, when, and with whom they interface. This planning from the beginning to the end improves productivity, reduces redundancy, and minimises rework. Project management shows the interrelationship of tasks, drives project schedules, and eases oversight of budget, risk, and quality. Project management decreases stress and miscommunications because all concerned have the same expectations and information about progress and/or delays. Let's look at a situation that could gain from formal project management.

One growing company faced the challenge of moving most of its manufacturing overseas, remote from the staff. This arm's-length manufacturing created major challenges and was a critical issue the company had to address. Almost 90 percent of its top products were now produced in Asia instead of the United States. This impacted every corporate function and required special attention from each function. The company now needed to bridge communications among finance, purchasing, engineering, product development, sales, and quality control with more structure, including formal project management.

When a company requires increased attention from every department, this calls for a new way to manage the interactions among the groups. Formal project management generally replaces informal project flow as organizations expand.

Another stimulant to implementing formal project management is expansion of product or service menus. In response to increased product demand and competition, a company concurrently upped the array of new products it developed and manufactured. This proliferation of new product types upset many employees because of their swelling work-loads. Management needed to tackle new project and personnel realities due to these unintended consequences.

Some companies formalize project management to shorten product development from original definition to market. This helps new product team members know how long particular tasks in the product-development cycle should take. It is easier to estimate and track the required person-hours for each task. This means timelines and schedules that coordinate with multiple functions can be accurately developed and communicated with minimal confusion.

Formal project management limits impromptu decisions being made with inadequate information or consultation. Project management drives decision-makers to gather enough specifics, from all people affected, to take appropriate action. When the determined action is well thought out, it avoids rework and employee frustration with ever-changing directives.

Project management also prioritises tasks so that individuals are not left to set their own priorities. Communicating priorities keeps employees safe and productive as they work on important tasks. Employees can also be confident that there are formal dates for project milestones and overall deadlines. This eliminates blaming and miscommunication that can occur when dates are informal or unwritten.

Management Workflow Processes

It is easy to see that process and project management ease communication for tasks and projects. Managers also need to set up ways to ease communication with and among their direct reports. You need to create management processes so that you can get work done with and through other people. These processes help your staff know what you expect. They also routinise communication so that everyone can depend on regular information exchange. Two important management processes are meetings and status reports.

Using Meetings to Optimize Communication

Well-structured meetings are recognized as a productive use of time. They can enhance understanding of responsibilities and build relationships. They can save time in the long run if people are clear on roles and level of authority as well as due dates. Here are some tips to increase communication during meetings you control:

— Weekly status/progress meetings, consistently done, contribute to two-way communication and benefit both direct report and manager. One purpose is to update the manager on progress made toward objectives, problems and how they are being fielded, and the employee's plan for the next week. This weekly checkpoint provides an opportunity for positive and redirective feedback and thus keeps the work on track. When the manager and employee talk weekly about the work, they are more likely to stay in sync and avoid surprising each other. Weekly meetings also improve time management because the employee and manager can save up nonurgent questions and reports until the meeting rather than constantly interrupting each other.

  Another purpose of a weekly meeting is that employees have regular access to their manager to build a relationship, gain clarification on expectations, and get needed resources. The employee can work independently between meetings and not be micromanaged because the manager is regularly kept informed.

— For project, product, or business strategy meetings, decide who should attend meetings to enhance cross-functional communication. Ensure that invitees are included by functions that need to be there, since staff time spent in meetings is expensive. Be sure all invitees know in advance what they are expected to contribute.

— Train and coach people to actively participate in meetings. Attendees should be held accountable for contributing information about their functions. Coach the person who remains silent in meetings and then complains later or waits until problems emerge. Sometimes these people are trying to avoid conflict. Help them learn how to address concerns as a business issue during the meeting to prevent larger conflicts and problems with others later on.

— Some individual contributors may have been raised in a culture that taught them not to express their opinion if more senior people, or people of higher education level, are present. Helping these individuals, whose contribution is so needed at meetings, to speak up may take some one-on-one conversations. Privately explore their reluctance to speak. Reinforce how important their ideas are to other team members. Ask them what you can do to make it more comfortable for them to have their thoughts included in the meetings. Be patient as they transition.

Using Status Reporting to Maximize Communication

Institute routine status reporting. This offers opportunity for mutual feedback to flow continuously. Weekly status reports can be online or e-mailed or brought to the weekly progress meeting. A high-level summary of goals and status is submitted with whatever level of detail the manager requests. This helps trigger regular positive and redirective feedback and coaching. These reports also create a record to which the manager can refer when assessing formal annual or semiannual performance reviews.

The reports create a sense of urgency on a weekly basis for employees to meet targets. They also reassure employees that they are heading in the right direction. Direct reports benefit from timely, job-related feedback and have an opportunity to give feedback to their manager. To elevate the importance of timely status report compliance, a measured objective could be added to goal setting on each individual's performance appraisal. Communicating status to management is a vital part of the employee's job. It is also a key management responsibility to know status as a part of effectively delegating.

Processes are common communication tools in companies. Standardizing the way a group does a job saves time and questions. Streamlining how work gets done saves money and reinventing the wheel. Processes provide the group with consistency and shared terms to discuss the work.

Project management affords the same benefits on a different scale. Effective PM drives project goals, schedules (including other groups' roles in the schedules), budget, and milestones or checkpoints. This planning takes the past into consideration in terms of planning for the future. By knowing how long various pieces of the work have taken in the past, a project manager is able to estimate how long similar tasks will take on the new project. The project is broken down into these tasks, which are sequenced and then scheduled.

The project plan is a wonderful communication resource for the team because everyone knows what is needed by when. It also aids managers in monitoring and controlling the workloads, work progress, and deadlines. These formal plans communicate project status to the team as well as to upper management. Strong project management can preclude misunderstandings and problems that crop up with people.

One successful company ran like a spinning top on the manufacturing side of the business, because it had procedures and processes in place. The employees knew exactly how to assemble the products and how long each part of the job should take. They knew who was next in the chain of getting the product built and why it was important to give it to them on time. However, on the engineering, sales, and product design side of the business, there were communication problems.

It is true that these functions are more creative in nature and offer more discretion to each professional in how to accomplish tasks. Perhaps that is all the more reason to formalise project management. Without formal interdepartmental project plans in place, they experienced classic miscommunications such as complaining instead of problem-solving. Conflicts intensified among departments and finger-pointing began. Groups blamed other groups. "Us-versus-them" thinking erupted. Time was wasted because a department would wait for information instead of being able to access it on a project management system.

Processes and project management plans help prevent these typical communication problems. And when they do occur, they are easier to describe in a factual way. Ideally an organization as a whole will have processes and project management in place. If so, learn them. If there are formal plans in place, you can develop and use project management within your scope of responsibility.

If you already possess PM skills, they will serve you well in setting expectations, developing fair relationships, and following up on achievement. PM assists in giving feedback because it enables a manager to stay focused on the work issue instead of the person. In coaching, you know what skills to help with. Using process and project management focuses conversations on the business issues and away from emotions, opinions, and personalities.

Project management starts with detailed scope definition and helps fend off scope creep. When the scope of the work creeps larger and larger, morale and productivity can dive. When scope is clearly defined and agreed upon upfront with upper management, there are business and relationship reasons for staying on course. If changes are requested, they can be discussed in terms of the impact on the whole project. Project activities are identified and clarified before the schedule is set. Project scheduling may include a critical path diagram showing interdependencies with other groups and specific timelines for passing the baton to them. This heightens the importance of meeting deadlines as everyone can relate each task to the project as a whole.

Delegating, observing performance, giving feedback, and coaching can be targeted directly to ongoing project documentation and status reports regarding specifications, budget, and timelines. Having processes for feedback, coaching, delegation, and listening is equally important.

BREAKING THE JUDGING HABIT

Judging is defined here as categorising a person by labelling, or describing him or her with a word or term. Characterising people with a name, or label, classifies them into vague groups, such as "the lazy people." may or may not agree on what "lazy" means, but one thing is for sure—a manager cannot fix "lazy." Sometimes judging is referred to as "name calling" or "tagging" or "giving a negative descriptor."

Judging reflects a person's opinion. It is not fact. Labelling someone causes tension between you and the other person and with others who may be aware of the tag. So why do we judge? Judging is a short-cut to communicating because it assumes others have the same definition of the label. That may or may not be true, but judging is a dead end when trying to address a performance issue and help people succeed.

Judgements can be positive or negative. Isn't it interesting that we are aware of when other people are judging us? Have you ever been "labelled?" Sometime in your life someone may have branded you with a descriptor that was repeatedly mentioned—usually to other people. It may have been something you liked, such as "prez" (for president), "the family writer," "the artist," or "the smart one." Or it may have been something you didn't like, such as "the scrag," "clumsy one," "idiot," "a klutz," or "self-absorbed." In this chapter, we address the latter type of labelling or making judgements—the kind people do not like. These judgements are impractical for team building and productivity. They cannot be solved logically as stated and they damage relationships and teamwork.

Negative Judgements Mean Unresolved Conflict

A clue that interpersonal conflict exists is when people judge someone in a negative light. When there is labelling or name calling, it is a fair bet that communication is not taking place and neither is conflict resolution. Oftentimes managers are upset or even angry with employees when they judge. Some typical comments from managers include: "She's got a self-esteem problem," "The younger generation has no work ethic," "The older generation has no technology expertise," and "She's Mt. Vesuvius."

Employees also make negative judgements. They may complain and blame their managers and coworkers. They often lament that their managers cannot, or will not, help them with their coworker problems. When they give up on their managers, they tell their friends.

A common employee comment is that coworkers bully them and the manager won't do anything about it. Or perhaps they think the manager bullies them. But what does that "bully" label really mean?

Typical Judgements

There are a number of judgements that are commonly used to indicate that the manager is not getting expectations met. Here are some labels repeatedly heard managers call their direct reports:

- Slacker
- Old dog (older worker)
- The kids (younger workers)
- Lame duck (getting ready to retire)
- Moron or idiot

Or sometimes managers use adjectives or other descriptors to allude to the problem they are experiencing with their employees. Here are some that are frequently mentioned:

- Short tempered
- Low self-esteem
- Bad personality
- Not committed
- Difficult
- Doesn't respect me
- Bad attitude
- Lazy
- Obnoxious
- Unreasonable
- Complacent
- Has tunnel vision
- Disinterested or doesn't care
- Overbearing
- Insecure

Unfortunately, some managers go as far as to use medical diagnoses, which they are not qualified to make, such as referring to direct reports as schizophrenic, bipolar, or depressed. How does this make the staff feel? What if the person they are labelling or some other coworkers actually suffer from these illnesses? It is never acceptable to call people by these terms, and it is not acceptable for managers to laugh when others do so.

When people judge each other, as in the above examples, the descriptions are vague and the problems unsolvable. The labels they call each other perpetuate their current perceptions. These self-fulfilling prophecies generate blame. Change in behaviour is not possible if no factual discussion takes place. Blaming prevents identifying and solving the *real* problem. It also can lead to managers feeling disappointment in or anger toward employees. This blaming occurs every day in the media, in politics, at work, and even in our personal lives. So if you find yourself blaming and judging, don't worry. It's a common habit and you can change it.

Did you drive anywhere or take a cab this week? By any chance did you call another driver a name? Driving is the simplest example to use because it is commonplace to get angry with other drivers occasionally. This happens when other drivers do not conform to communication symbols such as stop signs, double yellow lines, and even red lights. Or when they surprise you by changing lanes in an unsafe way. In short, the action they take doesn't meet your communication expectation (that they follow the rules of the road), or it surprises you (and maybe scares you).

What has driving got to do with workplace communication? It's an example of how people habitually and quickly respond when performance expectations are not met or when they are surprised or feel unsafe. On the job, when expectations are not met or there is a deadline looming, managers might worry that the work will not be done correctly or on time. That could threaten the security of the manager's main job—to get work done through other people. It's a common reaction to blame the other driver or, at work, the employee, because all the facts are not yet examined. You, and other managers, are not alone if you judge others. It's a widespread response.

Judgements hinder communication, relationships, and progress. They also inhibit managers from discussing the problem with the employee, because the judgement is not factual and not useful. Judgements also take managers off the hook—"there's nothing I can do; the person is 'like that,' that's all."

Many managers refrain from fixing the problems because they fear confrontation or disagreement. Sometimes they worry that they do not have the skill to handle an unpleasant situation. This is because they have not been trained to clearly state expectations and assess performance in a factual way. They may feel uncomfortable discussing undesired performance and giving appropriate feedback. Managers may feel vulnerable if they get into a conversation and are unprepared to handle potential opposition.

"Don't Judge Me"

Many TV comedies have had a character say to another, "Don't judge me." It is funny because judging is so common and most people have experienced it. So we laugh when the character says that. But in real life, most people do not appreciate being judged. They dislike being saddled with a name they can't shake. They bristle at being misunderstood. And they resent being labelled as "always" or "never" doing things, rather than having each specific action on each different day evaluated separately. Judging is not useful to managers or employees because it skips over the facts and leaps to name-calling.

When a manager labels a person, the manager may see the employee consistently through this lens ("slacker," "lazy," "poor work ethic," and so on). Then the manager may hunt for proof that the judgement is correct rather than trying to help the employee succeed.

What is more useful and solvable is to examine little chunks of the employee's behaviour rather than putting employees in boxes from which they cannot escape. Judgements are too vague and large to solve. But a problem that is stated as observed behaviours, rather than judgements or opinions, is solvable. It is a bite-sized problem to tackle rather than an overwhelming, infinite problem that erodes relationships.

Communicating performance discrepancies is simply a business transaction that needs to take place. It is easier to discuss performance when focusing on facts, not judgements. Having a factual discussion can cause an employee's behaviour to change because the manager has identified observable behaviours and an achievable path.

Analysing judgements and turning them into facts can also have surprising effects. Sometimes a manager sees that the judgement is off base when the facts are examined. Oftentimes a manager learns that the organization itself has prevented performance. Sometimes the manager has been the obstacle, by not setting clear expectations, not properly discussing changes, not giving regular feedback, or not asking process questions.

Judgements are common and the skill to deconstruct them can be easily mastered, helping you to be confident of your facts, learn the employees point of view, and determine alternative courses of action.

Easiness of Judging

We live in a judging world, so it is easy to fall prey to judging first and thinking later. One may not see very many excellent communication role models. Television is a medium that has the power to influence millions of people. This medium could teach viewers how to communicate well. The irony is that fiction and story require conflict to keep a reader or, in this case, a TV audience interested. Television news, commentary, coverage of political speeches, and even sitcoms frequently depict judging behaviours, and these become role models for how to act and how to communicate.

Millions of people worldwide watch TV news channels. It is easy to see how the news channels judge the people they report on. The commentators use a tone of voice tinged with amazement, disappointment, shock, or some other emotion that is supposed to be contagious to the viewer. Their choice of words shows their bias and tries to pull the audience to their point of view. Interviewers ask loaded questions that lead the interviewee in the direction the news station wants to portray—all to convince the viewer to judge the person on whom they are reporting.

Politicians choose words carefully to put their opponents in a bad light. They skillfully use semantics to sway their constituency to fall in line with their own feelings or with what will have the best marketing outcome. Instead of describing factual behaviour, many politicians cherry-pick certain quotes or deeds to back up their judging phrases. They might say something all encompassing like "she is a failure" instead of citing observable actions that resulted in one failure on one issue. Sometimes differing points of view are judged in a negative light instead of regarded as opportunities to look at all the facets of an issue.

Some of our funniest TV shows are satires with characters that demonstrate communication skills that are not helpful in real life. Without conflict, a story is boring. But in real life, conflict needs to be managed with skilful communication, or unhappy consequences can occur. At work, interpersonal conflict can lead to stress and lessen teamwork. Teams might experience discomfort, leading to missing deadlines or to not accomplishing the highest quality work.Strong managers who can step up to conflict, without judging direct reports, increase their credibility, solve problems quickly, and set up employees for success.

How to Untangle Judgements

Why use a process? A process helps you discover the underlying problem you are trying to solve, which is not apparent when judging/labelling. When judging, perception becomes the reality and the employee being judged is seen through only one lens—the label. No person performs every action the same way, and when we see him or her unilaterally as "a slacker," the true business problem may not get solved.

If you want to break a judging habit, you must first analyse the judgements you make. That will lead you to the facts of the situation and help you discover the real cause of the problem you are encountering. Only when you deal with observable actions or behaviours and facts can you dispassionately solve the problem. So how does one untangle judgements and solve the real problems?

At first we state the problem "as is," even if it is judging. It is important to capture the first impression. We then peel back the layers. Here is a four-step process you can use:

1. State the problem "as is"—your original definition of the problem (slacker, not committed, doesn't respect me, overbearing, old dog, etc.).

2. Identify observable behaviours and facts—what did you see and hear? Recheck those "facts" and eliminate any judgements. Keep re-checking until you have identified facts and observable behaviours— not opinion.
3. Brainstorm a list of alternative solutions or action steps.
4. Decide preferred solution/action steps.

Examples Using the "How to Untangle Judgements Process"

These eight examples are actual work problems (judgements) and solutions. The names of the managers have been changed to protect their privacy. Their stories may be different from yours, but you have probably heard other managers use the same judgements. Maybe you have even thought these judgements yourself. Your analysis and alternative solutions might be different because your situation differs. However, if you follow the four-step process, you will have a great chance at management success. This process will help you form the habit of sticking to facts and thus doing a better job of following up on employee progress, giving feedback, coaching, building relationships, and achieving your goals.

At first the managers specified their problems in these common judgemental, unsolvable terms:

A. Lazy lead analyst

B. Old dog foreman doesn't like change

C. Nitpicky and insensitive boss

D. Lame duck awaiting retirement

E. Weak link—employee or manager?

F. Controlling senior director

G. Hostile engineer

H. Employee milks assignment

When one creates a negative judgement about someone and gives him a label, it is easy to forget the details that led to the judgement in the first place. The solving is in the details, not in the label. Peel back the layers. Analyse the facts of the situation rather than targeting the person. This leads to discovering the root causes of the people problems. Once root causes are uncovered, logical action steps emerge. Solutions involve both following a structured process and preserving the relationship, or rebuilding it if damaged.

Now let's walk through the four process steps using the content provided by the eight managers about the A through H judgements. These examples of judgements will be redefined as facts. The alternatives and solutions that the respective managers decided to implement are also included. Perhaps you can get some ideas so you can untangle the judgements that plague you.

A. Lazy

1. *State the problem "as is."* The manager, Eliot, originally stated the problem as, "Lead analyst is lazy." To analyse what the judgement "lazy" means to Eliot, we move to Step 2.
2. *Identify observable behaviours/facts—what did you see and hear?* This step can be tricky. Sometimes what seem like facts are really more judgements. So you may need to keep peeling the layers. For example, Eliot said he observed the lead analyst abusing company time and not working to full capacity. But those are still vague judgements. When we kept asking, "What do you see and hear that makes you say that?" the real facts emerged:
   - She takes extended lunches and breaks, which are not reflected in her work hours' time sheet.
   - The capacity charts do not reflect the amount of work that should have been done in the hours

worked. As a lead person, her percent of the workload should be higher than the other employees.

Now we were getting somewhere. It is much easier to deal with these facts than with the judgements. Eliot's next attempt to describe the employees behaviours without calling her "lazy" resulted in calling the analyst "dishonest" and stating that the other employees were picking up the slack. Again, vague. So we kept digging, and Eliot got to the facts:

— The lead analyst delegates tasks that she is supposed to do herself and falsely claims to do work she's not doing. Capacity charts show proof of her lower productivity. She takes credit for those delegated tasks, claiming to have completed those tasks herself (the other staff dispute this).

— Other managers witnessed extended lunch and breaks. After facts have been presented to her, she denies them.

3. *Brainstorm a list of alternative solutions or action steps.* Eliot came up with this list:

   — Pull the job description and capacity standards information.

   — Review job expectations of this employee. Gather the capacity charts and other facts. Now give feedback to the employee.

   — Meet with employee to review policies (i.e., lunch hours), job expectations, and actual performance observations.

   — Clarify the lead analyst's understanding of job requirements by asking her to state what she thinks is expected of her.

- Make sure expectations are the same as the manager's.
- Set up action plans to meet expectations. Ask, "What specifically will you do to meet these expectations?"
- After she states her action steps, then ask, "What can I do to help you do your job?"
- Identify consequences for not meeting expectations. Document the conversation and use it as a baseline for future performance issues.
- Set up and hold twice-weekly job check-in meetings to make sure employee is on track with performance expectations. Discuss issues and build rapport.

4. *Decide preferred solution/action steps.* Eliot decided to follow all the action steps in Step 3 and then observe subsequent performance. Follow-up steps would depend on whether the analyst met expectations.
   - If the lead analyst meets expectations:
     - Employee keeps job and grows in skills and expertize.
     - Job check-in meetings might become less frequent.
   - If she does not meet expectations:
     - Document facts.
     - Consult Human Resources.
     - Counsel and begin disciplinary action according to company policy.

Eliot felt better once he had a plan instead of an unsolvable judgement. It may be difficult to converse about these issues with the employee, but it is a whole lot easier than confronting the employee with the word "lazy."

B. Old Dog

1. *State the problem "as is."* In this case, David, the manager, stated the original problem as, "The old dog does not like change."
2. *Identify observable behaviours/facts—what did you see and hear?* David said he was dealing with an older foreman who will only do what he wants to do. David continued that this foreman is an experienced person who only likes to do the "fun work." The foreman doesn't like to do housekeeping tasks, and he "milks the job," David reported. When we teased this information apart, we got to the facts.
   - The experienced foreman spends 85 percent of his time doing his familiar construction tasks (roadwork) at which he has expertize rather than new duties (industrial).
   - He should spend 80 percent of his time on the industrial work. Instead, he defers the industrial work to other employees (labourers). He doesn't finish the industrial work that he begins. He does complete roadwork assignments.
   - The foreman states, "I was hired to do the roadwork, not the other work," and "I don't like that other type of work."
   - "Milks the job" means he does roadwork almost full-time but does not do industrial tasks.
   - Industrial tasks are a new assignment in the last few months.

- The foreman has not had any training in the industrial tasks.
- The foreman, who had been a star performer until a few months ago, was getting blamed because the new assignments had not been fully explained and the foreman did not know how to do them because of lack of training.

3. *Brainstorm a list of alternative solutions or action steps.* David's list of options was to first determine if it was important that the foreman do industrial work instead of delegating that work to his direct reports. David needed more information to decide this. If it was only important that the industrial work get done, and not necessarily by the foreman, David would just confirm that new expectation with the foreman. If it turned out to be important that the foreman do the industrial tasks, then David listed these action step options:
   - Update the foreman's job description and David's expectations.
   - Acknowledge that the foreman was originally hired to do only roadwork and explain to the foreman that the job has changed now.
   - Discuss duties and expectations going forward.
   - Tell the foreman *why* it is important that he personally does industrial work rather than delegating all of it.
   - Tell him what percentage of time you expect him to do roadwork and what percentage is to be industrial. Tell him why each of these percentages is important and the impact on others.
   - Arrange dates for training on industrial tasks.
   - Get ideas for solutions from the foreman.

- Get agreement on what he will do from now on.
- State consequences of noncompliance.

4. *Decide preferred solution/action steps.* David decided to follow all the action steps and to start to document behaviour if the foreman refused to meet new expectations or attend training.

C. Nitpicky and Insensitive Boss

1. *State the problem "as is."* Kathy, the manager, said her boss is, "insensitive and nitpicky about performance."
2. *Identify observable behaviours/facts—what did you see and hear?* When we got talking about the situation, the behaviours and facts fell into two categories: The boss is new in his position, without adequate help from his own manager, and the boss needs help on how to deal with people.

   The fact that the boss is new in his position cast a different light on things. Kathy began to empathize with him instead of thinking he was insensitive. Maybe he did not have bad intentions, but lack of knowledge and skills. So Kathy listed these facts about the boss being new in his position:

- He is inexperienced as a manager of managers.
- His new management roles and the roles of his direct reports are not clearly defined.
- Unclear reporting relationships—no organizational chart or system.
- Unclear expectations—we don't know what he expects of us managers.
- He acknowledges the organizational problems, yet no solution has been determined.

Kathy realised that the boss had not received adequate preparation and organizational support for his newly expanded responsibilities. Managing managers requires broader communication abilities. She figured out that he needs help with how to deal with people. The observed behaviours and facts were:

- He has poor feedback skills: He criticises staff, yells, and does not give specific information about his expectations and what he wants the direct-report managers to do differently, and why.
- Managers have not observed him giving positive feedback to any of them when they do meet his expectations. They need to hear that they are on the right track—especially since there is so much uncertainty about the roles and expectations.
- He undermines the authority of direct-report managers with sarcastic remarks at staff meetings in front of our employees.
- He does not acknowledge employees. He passes people in the hall and gives no greeting.
- He rejects my ideas without giving his reasoning (he says, "I don't think it is important").
- He says, "You are paid to do the job."
- He disregards authority boundaries, criticises tasks and employee performance for which he is not responsible (our staff).
- He needs higher-level management and communication training.

3. *Brainstorm a list of alternative solutions or action steps.* Once Kathy quit labelling her boss as "insensitive" and examined the facts, she decided to take the initiative to improve the relationship. This would improve the work situation for the whole team. Kathy's list included:

- Meet with him one-on-one to formally discuss issues.
- Tell him of direct-report managers' needs for clarity on roles, reporting relationships/ organizational charts, expectations, and feedback delivered in a constructive way. Tell him how the clarification will impact the productivity and help him get his goals met.
- Give him feedback that direct reports want to improve working relationship with him and tell him of issues listed under Step 2 "observable behaviours/facts."
- Ask him for a meeting to clarify roles, responsibilities, and level of authority.
- Ask him to commit to identifying and solving the problems his direct-report managers are having with him.
- Tell his boss he needs direct on-site coaching by his own boss.
- Ask his boss to get him higher-level management and communication training.

4. *Decide preferred solution/action steps.* Kathy decided to start with all the action steps she brainstormed except the last two bullets, which deal with going to his boss. She might do that if she has to, but she chose to start with her boss in an effort to solve the problems effectively and build the necessary relationship with him. However, if he is not receptive to working with her to resolve these issues, Kathy will:
   - Tell him she is going to talk to his boss and invite him to join her. She will put it in positive terms of enhancing the working relationship of all team members.

- Suggest he invite all direct-report managers and his boss to a meeting to discuss and clarify expectations. She will get consensus in the meeting and document the decisions and results.
- Involve HR to mediate if they cannot resolve it.
- Check other positions within the company if it does not improve.

D. Lame Duck

1. *State the problem "as is."* Alexandra, the manager, first described the problem as, "The employee is a lame duck just waiting for retirement."
2. *Identify observable behaviours/facts—what did you see and hear?*
   - The employee is leaving in six months.
   - He is bored with his job.
   - There is no back-up person for his responsibilities.
   - He is a good employee—completes all work and does it well.
   - He has worked for company for over twenty years.

Alexandra agreed that she could not validate that the employee was "bored" with his job, since the employee never mentioned he was bored. "Bored" is a judgement. What was more useful were the observed behaviours that led her to say he was bored: Comes in late once every two weeks, leaves early once a week, and takes long lunches every other day. Now Alexandra had something she could work with—the employee was not complying with work-hour performance standards.

3. *Brainstorm a list of alternative solutions or action steps.*
   - Meet with employee and express her concern about how he ends his long-term employment with the company. Tell him she wants him to end his time on a successful note and that she will help him do that.
   - Set expectations about work-hour policy to be fair to all employees.
   - State consequences of not complying with policy and express her hope that he will comply.
   - Work together to create an exit plan that includes having him mentor people in his last six months so his institutional knowledge can be preserved.
   - Have him train one or two employees as back up on his job ASAP. These people will take over his responsibilities when he leaves.
   - After his years of contribution to the company, she will help him enjoy and celebrate his last six months.
   - Plan a retirement party with coworkers, if policy permits it. Otherwise, set up a lunch date.
4. *Decide preferred solution/action steps.* Alexandra decided to:
   - Follow all above action steps unless employee does not follow policy and expectations.
   - Treat him as she would any other employee by monitoring and documenting performance according to company policy if he does not comply, or if performance declines.

E. Weak Link (Employee or Manager?)

1. *State the problem "as is."* Ling said his problem was,

"How to deal with the weak link in the group when at least some members of the group know the employee is the weak link."

2. *Identify observable behaviours/facts—what did you see and hear?* When Ling tried to state observable behaviours/facts, he realised he had been calling the employee the "weak link," but that maybe he as the manager was the "weak link." He had not provided the employee with sufficient information to succeed. His list of what he had observed was vague. If he tried to talk to his employee, it would be like discussing cotton candy. It might look like a big problem, but if he and the employee bit into the problem, it would quickly disappear. He did not have concrete facts. Let's look at what he said so his action steps will make more sense:

   - Scope—it takes this employee the longest of all employees to absorb instruction.
   - Manager sets expectations and clarifies, yet the employee still misinterprets them.
   - The employee does not ask questions; he pretends to "get it."
   - When there is a definite deadline, he adheres most of the time.
   - Quality of output compared to others—he does not contribute as much as the other employees do.

3. *Brainstorm a list of alternative solutions or action steps.* Ling decided he had some homework to do. Here is his list:

   - Determine clear definition of expectations for this employee and put them in writing.
   - Tell employee the expectations. Ask him to restate what he thinks the manager expects of

him and by when. Ask him to send the manager an e-mail stating those expectations. Ask him to write exactly what he will do to meet those expectations.

- Get specific data on how long it takes the employee to absorb instruction. What do employees do to demonstrate they have absorbed instruction? What is the performance standard on how long it should take?
- Meet with employee and express the manager's desire for him to learn the job and achieve the objectives. Tell him the manager will add more structure to help him.
- Provide training or a buddy, if needed.
- Set milestones/check-in points for the work and dates to follow up on each milestone (project planning).
- Meet with employee on daily or twice-weekly basis depending upon his needs for help and the manager's needs to be sure he is on track.
- Explain impact on the team when quality is insufficient or deadline is not met. Do other workers have to cover for him?
- Keep up the regular one-on-one meetings.

4. *Decide preferred solution/action steps.* Ling decided to:
   - Try all of the above action steps.
   - If they don't work, he will begin the formal counselling process that the organization has in place.

F. Controlling

1. *State the problem "as is."* Mary Beth said, "Our senior director is controlling."

2. *Identify observable behaviours/facts—what did you see and hear?* Mary Beth was specific about the facts:
   - Three years ago her company had an audit that required corrective actions.
   - There were 1,200 open complaints three years ago, but they now have only 400 complaints.
   - The goal is to close complaints within thirty days of opening them, and the company is at thirty-nine days.
   - Senior management wants thirty-four days to be the maximum, and eventually for the company to meet the goal of thirty days.
   - The senior director calls every day to see how Mary Beth's department is doing regarding this goal. She also stops Mary Beth's staff in the hall, and even e-mails them asking for a progress date.
   - It took forty-five days to close complaints three years ago. Mary Beth's department has made significant improvement from three years ago, but the corporate image is not healed because complaint closings are not at thirty days. So instead of emphasising the progress they have made, the senior director constantly points out that they are not at the goal.
   - Currently, the closings are more than the openings, so throughput is over 100 percent. Mary Beth thinks that should count for something, but the senior director says the priority to look at is only to get the closings down to thirty-four and then thirty days.
   - The average closing takes twenty-four days, but the European region pulls the closings off average. So, the current average is thirty-nine days to close.

- Quarterly Trending Report is by product complaint and cause. They tend to be the same problems.
- The senior director constantly contacts Mary Beth and states that her team is not performing to the expected standard.

3. *Brainstorm a list of alternative solutions or action steps.* When Mary Beth got clear on the facts, she realised that she and her team wanted credit for improvement over the last three years but indeed they were not meeting the goals in front of them. The senior director was emphasising the importance of what goal Mary Beth's team must attain, rather than looking back at what they had accomplished in the past. Mary Beth decided to discuss the situation openly with the senior director. She planned to:
   - State to the senior director that she and her team are on board to meet the goal of thirty-four days and then thirty days to close. State what she and her team were prepared to do to meet that goal. Ask the senior director's opinion of what she thinks they could do differently to meet the goal. Tell the senior director she wants to work collaboratively with plans and follow-up on progress.
   - Set up frequent meetings with the senior director to discuss that sheets.
   - Ask the senior director to work with the European region to solve the problem they have with slow closing , since Mary Beth does not have the organizational power to do that.
   - Print a *progress* report showing progress percentage by quarter. On the quarterly report, show the regional breakouts, to show that the

European region is not complying and is dragging down the average. Compare current closings to past periods. Use bar charts (visuals) to highlight what the team did differently in each period.

- Prepare and deliver a quarterly formal presentation to the senior director rather than just e-mailing her the quarterly report. Discuss progress and plans for the next quarter during that meeting.
- Identify team training needs and organise the training.
- Invite the senior director to team meetings.
- Keep the senior director informed on a weekly basis of progress.

4. *Decide preferred solution/action steps.* Mary Beth decided to follow all the alternative action steps.

G. Hostile

1. *State the problem "as is."* Javier said the problem was "an engineer, who doesn't like to be questioned, becomes hostile and goes around the person he disagrees with."
2. *Identify observable behaviours/facts—what did you see and hear?* At first Javier's observations were judgements, so we kept defining what he saw and heard until he could describe observable behaviours and facts.
   - "Poor work ethic." This means the engineer comes in a half hour late and leaves fifteen minutes early twice a week.
   - "Violent outbursts." This means he shouts profanities.

- "Hostile when questioned." This means he rolls eyes, sighs, and walks out.
- "Unprofessional behaviour toward coworkers." This means he uses sarcasm or refuses to respond to them and forces his way into conversations.
- "Not a team player." This means:
  - Peer engineers object to working with him.
  - He seeks advice from others not involved with the project.
  - He is critical of others—offers negative feedback but not positive.

3. *Brainstorm a list of alternative solutions or action steps.* Javier's list:

- Ask Human Resources' counsel on the employee's behaviour related to shouting profanities to see if it is considered to foster a hostile work environment and to be harassment. Ask them whether to provide feedback from other engineers on how he is perceived. Take any action Human Resources advises.
- Review expectations of work-schedule tasks and projects.
- Review relevant company policies with him.
- Review expectations of acceptable behaviour toward peers and manager with him.
- Discuss expectation for open dialogue and working with team members.
- Discuss his observed behaviour, contrasting that with expectations.
- Explain impact of his behaviour on workflow and morale.

- Try to find root cause of his behaviour.
- Offer coaching and communication training classes to help him find proper ways to express ideas.
- Discuss consequences of continued behaviour, including company counselling process.

4. *Decide preferred solution/action steps.* Javier decided to start with Human Resources to discuss the shouting of profanities. He would then discuss the other bullet points with them and, if they agreed, follow all action steps brainstormed in Step 3.

H. Employee Milks Assignment

1. *State the problem "as is."* Deborah stated the original problem as, "the employee doesn't take the initiative. She only does what is asked of her and 'milks' assignments."
2. *Identify observable behaviours/facts—what did you see and hear?* This is what Deborah had noticed:
   - The employee closes Windows (computer applications) when manager walks by.
   - The employee meets all deadlines. However, she takes double the time needed to complete a task.
   - The employee takes one day to complete tasks that should take only a half day. Deborah previously did this job, but has not told the employee that this task should take a half day.
   - Employee does not inform Deborah when tasks are completed.
   - Employee does not ask for additional assignments/projects when she completes a task.

— Employee transferred from a subsidiary company.

Once Deborah completed this list, she realised how many assumptions she had made about how this new employee should perform. Deborah had not set clear expectations about how long jobs should take. Deborah needed to examine whether it was realistic to want the task completed in only a half day. After all, the employee did meet all dead-lines. Also, the employee is new to the organization and needs to be told about the expectation that she come to Deborah and ask for additional work. It may not have been an expectation where she worked before.

3. *Brainstorm a list of alternative solutions or action steps.* Deborah's list:

   — Determine how long tasks should realistically take. Just because Deborah did the task quickly does not mean that should be the measure.

   — Talk to employee about the length of time the project should take. Get her side of the story. She's a new employee so does she need training? More structured guidelines?

   — Discuss expectations that she get the task done in projected time allotted.

   — Discuss all other expectations about informing Deborah when tasks are completed and asking for more assignments.

   — Give shorter check-in times and follow-up at half day until no longer necessary.

   — Assign more work/tasks if employee needs more work.

   — Discuss adding a more challenging assignment.

   — Set up regular, periodic meetings/checkpoints/goals/status reports/deadlines.

4. *Decide preferred solution/action steps.* Deborah decided to follow all the action steps.

Through following the four-step process, you can replace judgements with facts and then easily determine a path toward a solution. As you saw in the examples, many times an employee was blamed when the manager was the organizational obstacle. It is common for managers following this process to realise that they may not have set clear or realistic expectations. The managers may need to provide resources, including training, in order for direct reports to meet the goals.

In the case of managing your manager, the same concept applies. Judging is frequently a misunderstanding. Once you examine the facts, it is often the "judge" who stands in the way of solving the problem. People who work with this process quickly and honestly examine who needs to do what in order to collaborate, achieve work objectives, and preserve relationships.

Word Choice

Once managers follow the process to discover the root of the judgement, they need to speak to the person they are having the problem with. Picking the right words can make the difference in whether the message is heard. The right words can also generate enthusiasm for collaborating and moving forward together to get the work done.

Words convey specific meaning. Managers are responsible for what they say. Since managers exert so much influence, whether or not they intend to, they must choose words carefully. It is important to be factual and friendly.

Words can include or exclude people, make them feel good or rile them up, and even assert dominance or invite collegiality. Selecting words appropriately and positively is one of the most essential decisions we make when we speak. The words we use can advance or impede communication about the work and the relationships. They show respect and courtesy, or the opposite. Consider the words in each of the following pairs and the connotation of each: smile/smirk, senior management/the suits, business trip/boondoggle, famous/ notorious, economising/cheap, curious/nosy, experienced/ over-the-hill, and youthful/ immature.

Poor word choice builds walls instead of bridges. Picking words ineffectively can make people feel discounted and unvalued. It can create or contribute to conflict, and be interpreted as insensitivity or lack of caring. It can lower employees' confidence and self-esteem. Words can place blame, create distrust, and shut down communication. And the person choosing unpleasant words can be viewed as being closed-minded.

Careful word choice can prevent people problems and establish an atmosphere of trust and respect. Neutral words or words with positive connotations show empathy and caring, create open communication, and facilitate conflict resolution. Positive words make it easy for the employee to hear your feedback and to feel welcome to give you feedback. When the relationship hits a roadblock, employees are more likely to work through the misunderstandings if they feel that, by and large, the manager is collegial and trustworthy, as demonstrated by his use of neutral and positive language. A trustworthy manager does not use judging terms or labels to describe anyone, up, down, or across the organization.

How to Handle Body Language Judgements

Besides using words, people can use their bodies, facial expressions, and tone of voice to insinuate judgements and put other people down. Imagine you and another speaker are up on the platform debating an issue in front of a large audience. You are seated next to each other. Every time it is your turn to speak, the other speaker lowers her head and shakes it slowly left to right. She scrunches up her nose in a way that brings her eyelids closer together rather than being open all the way. She smiles showing her teeth. She sighs audibly. We see this behaviour every day on news panels on TV, and you may see this in your office or at a meeting.

Even though it was not this person's turn to speak, she took the audiences attention away from you and your words by using body language. How do you react? Perhaps it rolls off your back and you don't care. Perhaps it upsets you. How do you interpret the body language? Do you say she disagreed with your message? Do you say she was rude? She smirked? She dismissed and discredited you?

One might have any of those opinions and they are just interpretations or judgements. They are not facts. The only facts are what we actually saw and heard happen as described in the first paragraph. The judgements may or may not be the purpose that person had in mind when she chose to react to your words using nonverbal communication. Acting on body language judgements will not advance relationships or get your message heard. You will have greater success staying with observed facts.

You have options while you are on the platform. You can ignore the nonverbal behaviour of the other person. This is what many managers choose to do with their direct reports. Sometimes it is appropriate, and sometimes the behaviour escalates until it bothers the audience (other teammates).

Let's assume you decide to address the nonverbal behaviour of the other speaker on the platform. If you choose to speak about your opinion/judgement, she will probably deny it and you will end up looking petty.

"Why are you being so rude?" you might say.

"I'm not being rude," she answers.

"Yes, you are," you continue. "You're smirking."

"You're wrong. I am *not* smirking. What's the matter—are your feelings hurt?"

Notice that you are not talking about the content of the debate, but the topic has now switched to your feelings. By now you might be plenty angry and easily distracted from the importance of your original message. You will not be winning the support of your audience. You will look like you do not exhibit grace under pressure. You may think people see you as a "victim" who can't handle the communication challenge.

Another option is to address the behaviour using only observable facts. This might get some information about *why* the person is using the body language and get an honest discussion going. Perhaps it will get you both back on track and focused about the work at hand.

"I noticed you shook your head 'No' and smiled when I made my point."

"Did I?"

You use neutral, open body language and silently wait for her to continue.

"Well, what you said about X was totally ridiculous," she says.

You ignore her tone of voice and concentrate only on the words she spoke. "What exactly did you find ridiculous?" you ask.

"I totally disagree with your comment about..."

"I'll present my research in a moment," you say. "But first let's talk about why you disagree."

Now you are back to debating ideas because you have facilitated a nonemotional discussion based on observable behaviours rather than being judgemental or letting the other person's judgements control your behaviour. You have stayed on message and can get results.

COMMON PEOPLE PROBLEMS

Besides judging or labelling people, there are other common people problems that are prickly for managers. A simple process is offered here to help you handle these types of problems. If you develop this simple skill for solving people problems, you will form a habit that will help you invigorate relationships and work collaboratively. This habit will help you achieve work results through others.

People problems *can* be solved, and it is the manager's job to handle these problems. Sometimes what seems at first to be a "people problem" is an opportunity to explore differing points of view. Multiple viewpoints can contribute to innovative and better products and services. Having different perspectives can help the team develop conflict-resolution skills, which strengthens the team. When coworkers are able to honestly state their views on the work, they develop trust in the working relationship and confidence that misunderstandings can and will be worked out.

Defining People Problems

"People problems" is a short-cut term many use to describe unresolved interpersonal conflicts, as opposed to mechanical, technical, or other work problems. Sometimes managers who are quick to resolve other work-related problems procrastinate about resolving work problems that they perceive are related to people. A manager might not like a direct report, or might judge him, Or a problem might exist between coworkers who report to the manager.

Sometimes there are elements of emotion involved and the manager isn't sure how to properly tackle the issue. Perhaps the manager wants to avoid confrontation or an unpleasant conversation. Or the problem is with the manager's boss or peer. The manager isn't sure how to approach a person she perceives as having equal or more organizational power because the stakes are higher. Oftentimes the manager just plain does not know how to define "people problems" as logical work performance issues to be solved by a rational process.

Conflicts can be about differences in opinion, traits, or beliefs. Sometimes a person thinks he is right and refuses to explore the other person's viewpoint. On the other hand, a person may lack confidence in his own ability or opinion or lack the capacity to defend his position without escalating conflict. Sometimes people fear looking bad or losing their jobs or reputations, so they choose not to be honest communicators. Others overlook the value and necessity of developing strong working relationships.

Causes

Misunderstandings and other communication problems among people at work are probably as old as work itself. How could it be otherwise? People have backgrounds and viewpoints that differ from those of others. Because of this, it is difficult to articulate meaning in a nonemotional way that others can understand dispassionately. This section will examine many factors that can cause communication problems.

Too Much Togetherness

The old adage "familiarity breeds contempt" means that

it is quite common for people who are together a lot—at home, at play, or at work—to become upset with each other. When people work closely together, there are bound to be misunderstandings and communication problems among them. Too much in-person contact might just be annoying, especially if a coworker has a habit we don't like. It is to be expected that people may become impatient with one another if they see each other frequently. Or they may take each other for granted and not make enough effort at communicating properly. They may misinterpret a message based on what it meant in the past when they worked on something similar.

Didier's cubicle is next to Pierre's. They have worked on projects together for over three years. Pierre has been the team leader and, from Didier's perspective, has imposed his way of approaching the project every time, supposedly because of time constraints. Today, Pierre asks Didier, "What are some alternative ways to approach this project? What do you think we should do here?" Instead of answering the question directly, Didier might use his past experience with Pierre and be cautious. Will he waste his energy if he spends time analysing the best approach and then Pierre does what he wants anyway? Has Pierre changed his leadership approach and does he truly want Didier's opinion?

Not Enough In-Person Contact

The opposite of too much togetherness is not seeing each other in person enough. Not being together in the same location contributes to many communication problems. Today many managers have direct reports who work at remote locations—at home, at a coffee shop, or at another office location. Other office locations can be in other cities or in other countries—even on other continents. These remote workers are connected to coworkers via the Internet. They work virtually, meaning technology links them together regardless of the geographic location or the time zone. Virtual teams collaborate and can be in constant contact worldwide.

If Ron works in Toronto and his direct reports work in Tokyo and London, he must develop a topnotch ability to manage by results, because he cannot observe what his team is doing on a day-to-day basis. Ron must also hone listening skills, because he will be working by phone when voice-to-voice communication is needed. Without seeing people in person, Ron will not have the benefit of observing nonverbal communication like body language. Most communication will be done via the Internet, which presents many opportunities for misunderstandings.

When the Message Sent is different from the Message Received

A typical communication problem is often categorized under "the speaker sends a message but the listener receives a different message." Why? There are many possibilities. Our life experiences frame our point of view, and our listener's life experiences form his outlook. Let's say Soula explains something to Kyle. Soula thinks she is perfectly clear, but Kyle hears a different meaning. Soula might be using jargon or vocabulary that Kyle is not familiar with. Or Soula might have a generational frame of reference (music, literature, historical events, technology, terminology, and so on) that differs from Kyle's orientation. If Soula has done the job a long time and Kyle is new at it, they have a different perspective on the work. There are many other reasons for this message sent and not being heard problem, including cultural differences and traumatic or major events that shape how a person sees things.

We could include e-mail under the category of a reader assuming a different message than the sender intended. Words and tone in e-mail messages are frequently misunderstood, and tempers flare. Sometimes the e-mail thread goes on too long, when a phone call could have straightened out the misunderstanding.

Not Knowing the Context

Sometimes we understand the vocabulary but not *why* people say what they say or do what they do. Their behaviour may seem out of place or it may not fit with the rest of the behaviour we have seen from them.

Not Listening

Another reason for miscommunication is lack of listening. It is easy to miss a person's meaning if one doesn't focus on the message.

"Personality Conflict"

Some people say they have a "personality conflict" with certain other people. They might say there is "bad blood" or "ill will" between them. Frequently these problems are just preferred behavioural styles and easily solved.

Downsizing Effects

When an organization is downsizing and running lean with fewer staff to do the work, it causes people to be stressed. They may worry about the quality of the work they can produce. Or they may be concerned about lack of time to accomplish their tasks or insufficient time to give appropriate depth in the analysis they need to provide for a task. The same thing can happen when companies are expanding with limited assets. Stressed managers managing frustrated employees can trigger miscommunications and problems among people who previously got along together.

When there is turnover or downsizing, personnel changes impact staff, who may have to learn to work with new people. If people leave, there is lost expertise and lost momentum. The people remaining may have to quickly learn new responsibilities and not be allocated time or resources for training. Stress can cause finger-pointing and lack of patience with each other.

Requests of Other Groups

Any time a manager makes a request of other departments for resources or to do work, the manager might not understand how the request impacts the other group. There may be a conflicting process or priority that needs to be ironed out. Both managers need to talk frankly about their needs and how they can work together to achieve the overall goals.

Uncertain Priorities

Organizational priorities that conflict and change rapidly cause miscommunication, hallway gossip, and uncertainty. This leads to stress and further communication problems.

Tips for Preventing People Problems

What should a busy manager do when faced with miscommunication, regardless of its cause? Besides using the process detailed below, there are some generic pointers a manager should keep in mind. Focus on the positive and assume peer managers and other colleagues have the best intentions. This will help shore up communication. Communicate frequently and consistently from team to team to create trust and reduce uncertainty. Tolerate others' stress and help them find a process to address their own concerns.

Helping them can buoy up the relationship. Some managers need to remind themselves to step back, breathe, and not judge others or be quick to say, "That's not right/fair." This time for reflection can provide the space for logical problem-solving. It is also important to accept that having people listen to you does not equal getting your way or the way you wanted it to happen. One of the key ways to prevent problems with people is to be specific about observed facts and behaviours versus labelling/judging them. Labelling can escalate people problems and cause new ones. It is indirect, ineffective communication and can be hurtful to people and their reputations. During times of stress, there is all the more reason to focus on preserving relationships and analysing problems in solvable ways.

Solving People Problems

Why use a process? A repeatable process helps you to develop a routine habit and saves you time whenever you encounter what you think is a people problem. You can easily discover what is bothering you, turn it into a clear work issue, and quickly move into action steps, just like you would do with any other business problem.

Here is a three-step process you can use:

1. State the issue
2. Define the problem and state the observable facts
3. Decide action steps

❖❖❖

9

PROBLEM-SOLVING THROUGH COLLABORATIVE CONVERSATION

The relationship is key to a successful collaborative conversation. The manager depends upon the relationship to set the environment for a frank, open talk about the work expectations and the observed progress toward those goals. When the relationship is in place, there is greater opportunity for honesty about what has occurred to date and how to continue or make midcourse changes so the employee can produce a successful outcome. Both people listen with greater give-and-take when the relationship is solid. They have more desire to understand the issues as intended by the other person. New information can be learned, and each person can redirect his or her focus, if needed. Process is equally valuable to the success of the collaborative conversation. When process is delineated, each person can lean on the structure to define terms and examine the alternatives for future action. This provides a common vocabulary and set of expectations, both of which facilitate collaborative conversation.

PARTNERSHIP BEHAVIOURS

For feedback to be absorbed and applied, a collaborative discussion, in which the employee explores the issue and best alternatives, yields the most ownership of solutions going forward.

Collaborative conversations require the intention to develop partnerships. The manager leads this by demonstrating partnership behaviours. Working toward win-win outcomes, or mutual success, is critical. Try to answer why changing the way the employee does things will benefit him in the short and long term.

Partners value the opinions of the other partner and appreciate their ideas on an equal basis. They recognize one another's talents, contributions, and knowledge. Associates are willing to learn from one another, listen to each other, and work as a team for mutual achievement. They share ownership of a goal.

An effective partnership builds on complementary knowledge, skills, and functional expertise. It creates common processes and vocabulary to enhance communication and goal accomplishment.

BUILDING TRUST AND CREDIBILITY

Collaborative conversations require trust. The manager needs to inspire trust before expecting to get it back. Sometime in your career you have probably heard someone say, "Trust me." What was your reaction? Words do not inspire trust. Management s do. Being consistent and doing what you say you will do are trustbuilding behaviours.

Most of us look for patterns of behaviours before we trust someone, and that trust grows deeper as we see consistent actions. When people align their words with their actions, they signal trustworthiness. Being honest and able to admit mistakes conveys open communication, which makes most employees more comfortable at work. Employees also look for indications that the manager is approachable, encourages and accepts their feedback, and stands up for them. Caring for the employees' best interests, fostering mutual success, and getting to know employees grows trust. The manager's competence and clear-cut goals trigger credibility. The ability to provide meaningful information, to follow through, and to hold people accountable generates credibility. The actual act of delegating extends trust to the employee and leads to faith in the manager's ability to assess the work and skills required to get it done. Removing obstacles to make the direct report's job easier demonstrates a willingness to work on a two-way street. Sharing experiences, showing commitment to the work and interest in employees, and adhering to high professional standards produce credibility.

Sometimes employees describe a manager who is credible as one who is willing to "roll up his sleeves and get dirty" to help employees in a crunch. When he does himself what he is asking employees to do, the manager engenders loyalty and collegiality. "We did it together" grows teamwork. Involving others in decision-making and asking for feedback and opinions demonstrates commitment to a "we" approach. This behaviour corresponds with a manager's intention to work jointly. Behaviour is what counts, not words or intentions. When a manager is always dependable, credibility and trust are built, and in turn grease the wheels of collaborative conversations and relationships

GIVING FEEDBACK

Feedback is telling people on a regular basis how they are doing in relation to the expectations and goals. This vital communication is honest and friendly and given with the intention of helping employees meet their objectives. It is an opportunity to keep the communication channels open. If delivered well, feedback contributes to relationship building. People want to know how they are doing in relation to the job at hand. They want to be affirmed when they are progressing. They want supportive help to redirect when they are off course, so they can achieve.

Feedback should be given immediately when is observed, in person or at least voice-to-voice. When it is given on a regular basis, the employee can feel confident that he or she is on the right track. This reduces stress and uncertainty. When given frequently, feedback becomes part of collaborative, ongoing conversations rather than a big deal. It is a habit and therefore expected and nonthreatening. When a manager chooses positive words, friendly (and nonjudgemental) tone of voice, and appropriate timing, feedback keeps people alert to what is important to the organization and how well they are fulfilling the expectations. This communication creates a comfortable, trustworthy environment because employees can trust that their performance will be observed and commented on with the intention of keeping them informed, developing their skills, and ensuring their optimum contribution to the team.

Types of Feedback

There are two important types of feedback: positive reinforcement and redirective. Both have a purpose and an appropriate use, depending upon whether or not the expectations are being met. Both are important communication tools.

Positive reinforcement feedback recognizes and reinforces specific desired behaviours. This feedback specifies positive behaviours that the manager wants to see repeated. Positive reinforcement feedback communicates that expectations are being met or exceeded and lets the employee know exactly what to keep doing.

Redirective feedback asks the employee to change, or redirect, her to better align herself to meet goals and expectations. This feedback is sometimes called corrective because it helps the employee adjust her approach early on so she can meet expectations and be suc- cessful. This type of feedback assists the direct report in knowing exactly what to do differently so she can change her actions.

It is important to give both types of feedback on a regular basis so employees can count on knowing their performance status. When employees expect both types of feedback, they understand feedback in the greater context of helping them achieve the goals and expectations. This enables them to view both positive reinforcement and redirective feedback as collaborative conversations.

Guidelines for Both Types of Feedback

When delivering either type of feedback, there are some guidelines. These general tips contribute to making the conversations collaborative and most effective.

- Feedback is an important communication tool, so give it in person or at least voice-to-voice (not by e-mail). E-mail is frequently misunderstood and can be blown out of proportion. Always link the feedback directly and explicitly to the expectation or goal and tell why that expectation is important. (Yes, even if you have said it many times before.)
- Be sure to discuss only one specific situation at a time—not "you always, you never, you often, or you usually," even with positive reinforcement.It is also important to identify precise, observable behaviour rather than making opinion or judging comments. A manager can also gather facts from project management milestones, plans, goals,

required processes, procedures, and other stated expectations. Facts clarify the communication and allow both the manager and the direct report to remain objective and results oriented. Judgements or opinions can lead to conversational detours so the main point gets lost.

— Be sure to give enough unambiguous and factual information to enable the employee to repeat the performance or make a requested change. While it's nice to hear, "Good job," it is insufficient information for a person to know exactly what that means. Similarly, comments such as, "Almost there" or "Not quite" do not identify what is expected and what the employee needs to change.

Feedback is never about the person. It is about the — action or inaction related to the expectation. To keep the talk collaborative, be supportive in words and process. Keep building the relationship between you and the employee. Using a friendly, neutral tone of voice conveys your intention to help the employee succeed. Be sure to generate excitement for the person's potential to achieve the goal—frame the feedback in a positive context.

DELEGATION

Delegation is assigning a task or project for which you are accountable but do not necessarily have to do yourself. It is trusting someone else to accomplish work and obtain a specified outcome, with certain performance standards. Level of authority varies for each responsibility and must be clearly identified before the employee starts work on the assignment.

Delegating work with low opportunity and high boredom will not build camaraderie. There should be positive reasons for delegating— getting more work done, seeking more viewpoints and employee development, or making time for managerial tasks. Another measure to consider is what salary level is appropriate to the task. A manager must also decide how to distribute the work to the team so each person can balance his or her workload.

Criteria for choosing the person to whom to delegate varies and must be clearly delineated. What is the nature of the task? What knowledge and skills are required to successfully complete it? How much time is available? Can I train someone? Can this be a development opportunity for a particular employee? Do we need someone who already has the experience on this or similar tasks because of criticality of the project, visibility, or time constraints?

Determining required skills and experience for a task or project is essential. The manager can identify who has the necessary capability to minimise the manager's involvement in the tasks. Or, the manager can delegate the task to someone who needs to develop those skills. This will necessitate proper training and more coaching but bring a return on that investment over time.

When to Delegate and How to Trust?

Managers are often concerned about how to balance their time and responsibilities and those of their direct reports. Sometimes they wonder what to delegate and when. You cannot delegate if you do not have the authority over the task or project..

After you decide how much of the task and what level of authority you will delegate, decide how much to delegate to each individual.

Chunk it down into pieces if you are not comfortable delegating the whole task or project. You can keep parts and parcel out parts to one or more people.

Then, pick the correct people and trust them to drive it to completion. But, one of the ways to increase trust is to set checkpoints and monitor progress along the way. So trust your intuition. What does your intuition tell you about this particular task or project delegated to this particular person? What information will you need and when will you need it to feel comfortable that the job is getting done according to specification, within budget, and on time? Schedule progress check-ins accordingly. Maybe your weekly progress meeting is sufficient and maybe not. A manager does not need to apologise for needing to know status. As time goes on, you might decide to stretch the checkpoints further apart. Trust grows, dependent on consistent delivery, not on how much we like people.

How to Increase Collaboration When Delegating?

Some managers worry about the way they delegate. They think they are too authoritarian in their approach and get resistance from their employees because of it. They have asked, "How can I be more diplomatic in the way I request that something get done?"

One thing to remember is that delegation is not really a request—it is an assignment. A confident manager might word it as a request knowing that will increase collegiality and the employee's ownership of the task. That approach can work quite well to maintain good working relationship. But it takes a self-assured manager who has established a collaborative relationship to make it work.

Similarly, managers are not asking for a favour when they delegate work. It is the manager's job to decide who is best suited to do what by when. Sometimes managers who have well-built two-way relationships with employees will delegate by saying, "Can you do me a favour?" because they know the person will say yes and it is the nature of their relationship. It keeps things feeling more reciprocal. In fact, their employee might say the same to them, "Can you do me a favour?" when they need resources or help to get a project done. It all depends upon the relationship. These phrases are ways to hold collaborative conversations in which both people view themselves as colleagues trying to meet the shared goals. They do not look at the organizational hierarchy when they work together. The energy flows. Managers who have not yet developed strong relationships might find themselves in the situation of one manager who intended to "request" something but actually displayed an authoritarian demeanour.

To increase collaboration, try these tips:

- Be confident that delegating is part of your job.
- Use a neutral, friendly tone of voice.
- Tell how the tasks fit company goals and why they are important.
- Tell why the delegatee was specifically selected.
- Invite questions.
- Listen.
- Understand the employee's style and adapt yours.
- Be respectful in language, tone and volume of voice, and body language.

Benefits of Delegation

Managers report numerous benefits of delegation to both themselves and to the delegatee. Here are some reasons to delegate for the greater use of each person's talents and abilities.

Benefits to the Manager

The more a manager delegates, the better he develops that skill. This prepares him for a broader scope of responsibilities. Not only does the manager enhance delegation skills, he builds other managerial skills by focusing on higher-level tasks. The manager can focus on long-term strategies and planning, for example. This creates a more efficient use of time for the whole team.

Because delegation frees up time, the manager can attend to more advanced work that demands and improves managerial skills. Having these skills leads to success as a leader. Part of leading is having time to enhance training and mentoring of staff, so the effect is cyclical.

Frequent delegating helps managers build trust in people because direct reports have the opportunity to demonstrate that they can and will deliver results. A pattern of accomplishment emerges and shows that delegating pays off. And the manager gets a chance to learn about the skills and abilities of his employees. This can lead to delegating more complex work.

The more the direct reports have an opportunity to showcase their knowledge and expertise, the more strengthened and motivated the team. Teamwork is built when many hands are working collaboratively toward shared goals. The more team members that a manager delegates to, the greater the diversity of ideas and new perspectives. Inviting fresh perspectives leads to innovation and process streamlining. Eliciting full team involvement increases commitment and enjoyment for everyone.

Delegating leverages the technical skills of individual contributors, who are often better matched to the technical demands of the project than the manager. In addition, delegation offers cross-training, which is in the best interest of the business. It also ensures productivity when the manager is away and increases the readiness of employees to step up to new accountabilities and to be potentially promoted from within.

Delegating provides variety for both managers and employees when they take on different tasks. It also offers efficient use of skills and talent appropriate to the task. This should have the effect of productivity and higher output for the team, perhaps leading to increased revenue.

When a manager confidently delegates, it demonstrates achievement of the overall management responsibility to develop others and get ideal results with and through direct reports. It improves the organization by creating a well-knit, smooth running, collaborative team. Delegation trains future leaders, which strengthens the fabric of the organization. And managers find they can discover "diamonds in the rough" when they give direct reports opportunities to excel.

Benefits to the Direct Report

When the manager trusts an employee with new, perhaps higher-level work, it also engenders the employee's trust in the manager. Trust flows reciprocally. Trust and increased levels of responsibility empower direct reports and offer them more visibility in the team and organization.

Trust builds rapport and a feeling of working "with," not "for." This collegiality often makes direct reports feel valued and useful. It can motivate and engage employees. It can also secure buy-in, project ownership, and accountability.

Sometimes these delegated tasks offer networking opportunities, which benefit the individual as well as the whole team. Advanced-level tasks provide the opportunity to do something new, develop new skill sets, prove knowledge in another area, and get recognition. The tasks or projects may present the opportunity for the employee to make recommendations, do things in his own way, or demonstrate his unique expertise. This proven success enhances employees' qualifications for broader responsibilities and promotion. The direct report might develop the reputation as a "go-to" resident expert or subject matter expert (SME). He may also earn the skills necessary to fill in or be the backup replacement for the manager.

As people learn new tasks and progress in abilities, they gain a sense of accomplishment and job satisfaction. They may experience a heightened confidence level in their knowledge and value to the organization. Staff morale is enhanced with an increased sense of competencies.

Why Are Managers Reluctant to Delegate?

Managers recognise the many benefits of delegation; why, then, is it so difficult to delegate? Managers can come up with many barriers to delegating. They say they are reluctant to delegate for personal reasons of their own and for reactions they suspect their employees *might* have.

Personal Reasons

One reason some managers do not delegate is because they fear they will lose their technical skills. They want to keep them honed, especially to be prepared when there is an economic downturn. Also they may feel that they are better at the old job than they are at the new one if they are a new manager. Since they were probably promoted because of outstanding technical skills, they may feel, correctly, that no one on the team measures up to the expertise they achieved. This means it is easier for the manager to do it herself because she can do it faster or better than any of her direct reports. Some managers fear that time will be wasted on rework. This may be the case until direct reports come up to speed on the new responsibilities. But the manager will end up doing the task forever if she does not delegate, and this will take a lot more time than developing an employee.

In the short term, delegating may take more time for the manager than doing it himself. The manager may think it will be more stress to delegate because he will have to set and clarify goals, decide and communicate timelines, train, follow up, and give feedback. There may be communication difficulties, and he may think there is no time for questions or instruction. If the manager has time-management issues, the manager may think he has no time to spend with direct reports. We are all limited by the time available, but a big part of the manager's job is to spend time with staff and help them grow and produce work.

Some managers doubt their own abilities. They may feel a sense of insecurity. Some say they have weak training skills and it is time-consuming to train direct reports. Others say they are unskilled in how to prioritise and properly decide what to delegate and to whom. These skills can be developed in training classes or by coaching from the managers boss. Reaching out to managers who are more experienced in delegating easily solves lack of current ability.

Fear prevents some managers from delegating. They may fear loss of control, that quality and standards might dive, that employees do not have the competency, or that they cannot trust others to do the work. Still others are afraid that a strong-minded employee will intimidate them. Experience will nurture confidence to overcome these fears. It is a bit like swimming. You cannot learn to swim until you get into the pool.

When managers lack authority or are unsure of their level of authority, they rightfully avoid delegating. If you lack upper management support and guidance this must also be discussed immediately with your manager. Managers cannot successfully delegate without having authority in the first place and knowing that management will back them up.

Reluctance to delegate can be caused by a lack of resources and qualified, competent employees. Sometimes a manager is concerned about adding stress to employees and does not want to overload or over-whelm them. Some managers feel guilty, or do not want to be perceived as lazy or taking the easy way out.If a manager got burned in the past when an employee did not come through with a completed assignment, she may not want to delegate. Or, the manager may find it difficult to balance check-ins and oversight with leaving direct reports alone to work independently.

Virtual and remote delegation requires more complex communication. The work may be 24/7, 365 days a year. Lack of face-to-face contact is challenging when the manager needs to discuss and clarify delegation issues. In addition, there are time barriers when managing people remotely around the world. Language and cultural barriers also play a part in reluctance to delegate when managing remotely or virtually. Sometimes e-mail delegation is the only option, and e-mail can easily be misunderstood or ignored.

A manager who worries about not getting personal kudos after delegating tasks need not be troubled. If a manager is a skilled delegator, his staff will accomplish the goals and meet all the specifications. This is the manager's true responsibility, so the manager should receive recognition for succeeding in managerial work.

Concerns About Employee Opinion

Some managers are disinclined to delegate because they imagine the employees might view the delegation negatively. These managers think employees may not be committed enough to the manager or the organization. Or they think direct reports might resist accepting more work; another assignment could be perceived as punishment. Employees might say, "It is not my job." Employees could think that there are unequal workloads among team members.

Assigning certain plum tasks could generate comments about favouritism and cause dissension among team members. On the other side of the coin, unimportant, tedious tasks could demotivate employees, and they could think the boring task assignment is not fair. Managers say that employees fear getting an increased workload on a continual basis if they agree to take on one new task—especially if they do it well.

Delegatees may think they do not have the skill or experience to do a certain task and fear making mistakes or even failure. They may worry about lack of support or have an opinion that the manager is pushing work down on them. Direct reports might have concerns that the priorities will change midstream and the work will be for naught.

All of these delegatee concerns can be controlled by a skillful delegator who follows a process and keeps communication channels open. If direct reports think they will do all the work and someone else will get all the credit, assure them you will provide them with plenty of positive recognition when the task is completed as required.

Challenges When Delegating

Managers mention many challenges when delegating. These include:

- Virtual or remote delegation (staff work on other continents, countries, cities, sites, or at home, rather than physically where the manager works)

— Language barriers
— All communication being via e-mail and phone because of location
— Time needed to provide support when delegating to a "green" staff
— Knowing how to delegate to different skill levels
— Work that changes and grows daily
— Allowing others to do it their way, which may be different than the manager's way
— Knowledge transfer challenges
— Employees who are more experienced than the delegator

Hallway Delegation

More formal delegation, using a process, will assure the most success for the majority of assignments, especially for long-term project work. This is because of the time the delegator takes to clarify exactly what is and what is not desired. Using a process provides the logical steps that remind a manager to consider all the parameters, such as the interdependency of tasks and projects with other coworkers or departments. What happens to the big-picture goal if this delegation is made? Using a process gives the manager and employee time to clarify specifics and ramifications, clear the air on any concerns or workload issues that require reprioritising, and prevent people problems through making it a collaborative conversation. If a manager is going to entrust someone else to achieve results for which she is accountable, the manager can get the best results by following a rational process rather than spontaneously assigning accountability in passing.

Corporate culture must also be taken into consideration in terms of how work is usually delegated.

But, sometimes corporate culture must be challenged. Just because it is the usual way of doing things does not mean it provides the best communication, the most cost-effective method, the least-confusing way, or the best way to ensure all projects coordinate with each other. "We have always done it this way," does not guarantee the best outcome or the most effective way to reach a goal.

At times, every manager must squeeze out as much quality work with as few staff members as possible. It is essential that delegation starts with communicating clear expectations so both manager and report have the same understanding of the expectation the first time. Everyone needs to save time.

A manager must be sure of the interdependencies of how this delegation relates to other teammates, projects, tasks, teams, and departments. This requires using a systematic process and not assigning work without considering the possible effects.

DREAM Delegating Process

The DREAM process described gere helps increase clarity and minimise stress for both the delegator and the employee accepting the assignment. It is imperative that managers do all they can to preserve employee commitment in times when every person is asked to do more. It may take a little time to learn the process in the beginning, but it will save you time in the long run because it is a repeatable process that ensures as much clarity and collaboration as possible.

1. Decide What and Who
   - What task/project or portion of a project are you delegating?
   - To whom are you selecting to delegate and why?

- What will you tell the delegatee about her skills and experience as they relate to the delegated work?

2. Resources
    - What help will you provide the delegatee to do the assignment?
    - What access to subject-matter experts, budget, equipment, staff or temporary staff, and materials will be available?
    - What will you do to ensure employee gets those resources?
    - How and when will you give feedback on progress?
    - What kind of coaching and support will you provide the delegatee?
3. Expectations
    - What is the goal of the work?
    - What exactly does a successful outcome look like?
    - What will a high-quality job look like in terms of quality, quantity, timeliness, and behaviours that contribute to teamwork?
    - Are there other desired results, such as innovation and creativity?
    - What will the evaluation criteria for success be?
    - What is the budget and specified criteria?
    - What is the deadline?
    - What are the potential problems and opportunities? If problems occur, what support will be available? Who is the proper person to contact?

- What happens if critical performance standards are not met on time, within budget, and according to specified criteria?

4. Authority Level
   - What level of authority does the delegatee have on this task or project? This can range from complete autonomy (she makes all the decisions and tells you what she has done) to low authority (she does it your way) or anything in between (such as making a recommendation and asking you before acting). Be very specific.
   - How much discretion does the delegatee have about how to do the task or project? Be specific to prevent people and project problems.
5. Monitor with Milestone Reporting
   - What are the milestones or check-in points along the way?
   - At what events or dates will the check-ins be?
   - Is there a computer system the employee must update?
   - What feedback do you want to receive in between checkins? How do you want to receive it—verbally or in writing?

What to Delegate?

What to delegate depends on a number of variables. Every manager must decide continually what is appropriate to delegate depending on the task, workload, deadlines, priorities, and availability of people with the needed skills.

What could you delegate to your team right now? A list of possibilities follows. Other managers have said they could delegate these responsibilities, and maybe this list will trigger ideas for your situation:

- Data entry and data recording on reports
- Running some meetings
- Attending some meetings for the manager
- Routine reports
- Technical troubleshooting
- Safety meeting presentation
- Discovering or researching solutions to problems
- Scheduling
- Certain client interactions
- Orientation and training for new employees
- Preparing and delivering presentations
- Case reports for legal arbitration
- Inventory planning
- Engineering drawing requests
- Weekly report on invoice data
- Coordinating with purchasing department

What Not to Delegate

Your situation may vary, but here are general guidelines for what not to delegate:

- Any assignments you don't have full authority on
- Work with legal consequences for the organization
- Confidential activities
- Monitoring and evaluating staff's work
- Final budgeting decisions—although you might ask for input
- Running staff meetings
- Final decisions on strategic planning, goal setting, developing a vision
- Audits

LISTENING

Listening is perhaps the greatest skill an expert communicator can develop. This capability can make the difference between communication and miscommunication, and between enhancing relationships and harming them.

Managers are responsible for the success of the communication. Listening intently—to be sure you understand what the speaker means—is a part of all communication. It takes a few minutes of concentrated attention, but it can save an immense amount of time. If you and your team are under pressure because of leaner staffing, listening heightens your chances of success. It is critical to understand the messages the first time to save time.

Listening is an integral part of developing relationships. A manager cannot show she cares about people and earn their trust if she does not fully listen to them. Real listening builds credibility and trust, which are necessary for influence and persuasion.

Listening is crucial when delegating and clarifying expectations. Managers must communicate back and forth with direct reports to ensure that both manager and employee have the same understanding of the goals or informal expectations. How could managers give feedback without listening to the employees perspective? Expert coaches have highly developed listening skills since coaching is a collaborative conversation. In fact, any collaborative conversation implies that both parties are listening to one another.

Tips for Collaborative Listening

The listener's body language lets the speaker know that he has the listeners attention. Eye contact—not eyes glasing over, but genuine, attentive eye contact—is the first indication of listening. Open body language, where the manager faces the direct report with arms open—not crossed, not working on a handheld or a computer, and not fussing with papers— shows it is the employee's turn to talk and that what the employee has to say is valued. Other listening body language consists of facial expressions and head movement. The listener might use such facial expressions as a slight frown or a general confused look in the eyes if she does not understand. Or the listener might nod her head slightly to show that she does understand.

Comments such as "Uh-huh," "Hmmm," "Yes," "I see," and "Oh?" said in a neutral, friendly tone of voice are nonjudgemental and noncommittal and encourage the speaker to continue talking. They are indicators that the listener is interested in hearing more detail about this topic.

Clarifying What We Think We Heard

Another valuable act of listening is clarifying what we *think* we heard. This is done by restating comments the direct report makes, asking clarification questions, and paraphrasing what we thought we heard. This way we can be sure we understand the real meaning of what the person meant to say. It does not necessarily mean we *agree* with what the person said. It does mean we respect her enough to let her know her message has been received the way she wanted it to be heard. This is easy to do if we take the time to clarify, rather than tuning out what has been said or accepting it at face value.

1. *Restate comments.* When you use the speaker's own words, you prove that you are still listening and want a more in-depth explanation. These comments reflect what the direct report says or implies. These comments can be used to draw out more information and to establish empathy.

2. *Ask clarification questions.* When you want to probe deeper to clarify your understanding of what the direct report really means, request clarification.
3. *Paraphrase.* Paraphrasing is similar to restating, except that in paraphrasing you use your own words instead of the speaker's. Also, listeners often paraphrase using a question instead of a statement. The purpose of paraphrasing is to be sure you understand what the direct report meant—by saying it a different way. Especially when used in question form, paraphrasing is collaborative because it invites the speaker to continue.

Listening is easy if a manager makes a commitment to listen. Sometimes you will be too busy to listen. You might be solving a crisis, be on a deadline, or have an appointment. If you do not have time to listen, say so. Tell your reports that what they have to say is important to you and you want to give it the attention it deserves. Invite employees to come back at a specific time when you will be able to concentrate fully on their message. When you are ready, here are four tips:

1. Clear all other thoughts and focus only on the person.
2. Eliminate thoughts of yourself—no advice, no "me too."
3. Use open, listening body language
4. Clarify what you think you heard by restating, asking clarifying questions, and paraphrasing.

When managers use this easy process instead of assuming they know what the speaker means, amazing relationships and understanding about the work emerge. When managers do not interrupt, multitask, or act hurried, but actually listen, rework is reduced and better products are produced.

❖❖❖

SELECT READINGS

Adam Kahane and Peter M Senge, *Solving Tough Problems: An Open Way of Talking, Listening, and Creating New Realities*, Berrett-Koehler Publishers, 2007.

Arthur Whimbey, Jack Lochhead and Ronald B. Narode, *Problem Solving & Comprehension: A Short Course in Analytical Reasoning*, Routledge, 1999.

Dawson, R. *Make the Right Decision Every Time*, Nicholas Brealey, London. 1994.

Donald Treffinger, Scott Isaksen and Brian Stead-Doval, *Creative Problem Solving: An Introduction*, Prufrock Press, 2006.

Edward Zaccaro, *Becoming a Problem Solving Genius*, Hickory Grove Press, 2006.

Greg Z. Fainberg and Ms Ruth Tearle, *How to solve just about any problem: Timeless practices for solving problems better*, CEXINO, 2010.

Greg Z. Fainberg and Ruth Tearle, *How to Solve Just About Any Problem: Timeless Practices for Solving Problems Better*, Crown Business, 2010.

James M. Higgins, *101 Creative Problem Solving Techniques: The Handbook of New Ideas for Business*, New Management Pub Co., 2005.

Janet E. Davidson and Robert J. Sternberg, *The Psychology of Problem Solving*, Cambridge University Press, 2003.

John Adair, *Decision-making & Problem Solving Strategies*, Sunday Times Creating Success, Kogan Page, London and Philadelphia, 2007.

Ken Watanabe, *Problem Solving 101: A Simple Book for Smart People*. Portfolio Hardcover, 2009.

Mayer, R. E. *Thinking, problem solving, cognition*. New York: W. H. Freeman and Company. 1992.

Michael Michalko, *Thinkertoys: A Handbook of Creative-Thinking Techniques*, Ten Speed Press, 2006.

Morgan D. Jones. *The Thinker's Toolkit: 14 Powerful Techniques for Problem Solving*, Crown Business; Revised edition, 1998.

Morgan D. Jones. *The Thinker's Toolkit: 14 Powerful Techniques for Problem Solving*, Crown Business, 2009.

Patrick Fanning and Matthew McKay, *Successful Problem Solving: A Workbook to Overcome the Four Core Beliefs That Keep You Stuck*, New Harbinger Publications, 2002.

Paul Zeitz. *The Art and Craft of Problem Solving*, Wiley, 1999.

Sandor Lehoczky and Richard Rusczyk, *The Art of Problem Solving, Vol. 1: The Basics*, AoPS Inc.; 7 edition, 2006.

Scott Fogler and Steven E. LeBlanc, *Strategies for Creative Problem Solving*, Prentice Hall, 2007.

Tim Hurson, *Think Better: An Innovator's Guide to Productive Thinking*, McGraw-Hill, 2007.

Tony Proctor, *Creative Problem Solving for Managers: Developing skills for decision-making and innovation*, Routledge, 2010.

Tony Proctor, *Creative Problem Solving for Managers: Developing Skills for Decision-making and Innovation*, Taylor & Francis, 2007.

Other Books on

MANAGEMENT